Nelson English

D0259519

Developing Non-fiction Skills

4

BOOK FOUR

John Jackman   Wendy Wren

Nelson

Contents

Anne Frank's Diary

During the Second World War, the Nazis persecuted Jewish people, rounding them up and imprisoning them in concentration camps. One Jewish family – the Franks – had fled Germany for Holland to escape the Nazis. However, the Nazis had occupied Holland and Jews were not safe. On 9th July, 1942, Anne Frank, aged 13, her sister, Margot, and their parents, along with another family – the Van Daans – went into hiding in a secret apartment in the upper two floors of Mr Frank's office building. They remained there, undiscovered, for more than two years. Dutch friends kept the secret and smuggled in supplies. While they were in hiding, Anne kept a diary. Here are some extracts:

<u>Thursday, 9th July, 1942</u>

I will describe the building ... There is a small landing at the top ...

The right door leads to our 'Secret Annexe'. No one would ever guess that there would be so many rooms hidden behind that plain door painted grey. There's a little step in front of the door and then you are inside.

There is a steep staircase immediately opposite the entrance. On the left a tiny passage brings you into a room which was to become the Frank family's bed-sitting-room, next door a smaller room, study and bedroom for the two young ladies of the family. On the right a little room without windows containing the washbasin and a small W.C. compartment, with another door leading to Margot's and my room. If you go up the next flight of stairs and open the door, you are simply amazed that there could be such a big light room in such an old house by the canal. There is a gas stove in this room ... and a sink. This is now the kitchen for the Van Daan couple, besides being general living room, dining room, and scullery.

A tiny little corridor room will become Peter van Daan's apartment. Then ... there is a large attic. So there you are, I've introduced you to the whole of our beautiful 'Secret Annexe'.

Wednesday, 13th January, 1943

Everything has upset me again this morning …

It is terrible outside. Day and night more of these poor miserable people are being dragged off, with nothing but a rucksack and a little money. On the way they are deprived even of these possessions. Families are torn apart, the men, women and children are all being separated. Children coming home from school find that their parents have disappeared. Women return from shopping to find their homes shut up and their families gone.

The Dutch people are anxious too, their sons are being sent to Germany. Everyone is afraid.

Above: *The entrance to the secret annexe.*
Left: *Anne Frank*

Monday, 26th July, 1943

It was about two o'clock … when the sirens began to wail … we had not been upstairs five minutes when they began shooting hard, so much so that we went and stood in the passage. And yes, the house rumbled and shook, and down came the bombs.

I clasped my 'escape bag' close to me, more because I wanted to have something to hold than with an idea of escaping, because there's nowhere we can go. If ever we come to the extremity of fleeing from here, the street would be just as dangerous as an air raid. This one subsided after half an hour …

That evening at dinner: another air-raid alarm! It was a nice meal, but at the sound of the alert my hunger vanished … "Oh, dear me, twice in one day, that's too much," we all thought, but that didn't help at all; once again the bombs rained down …

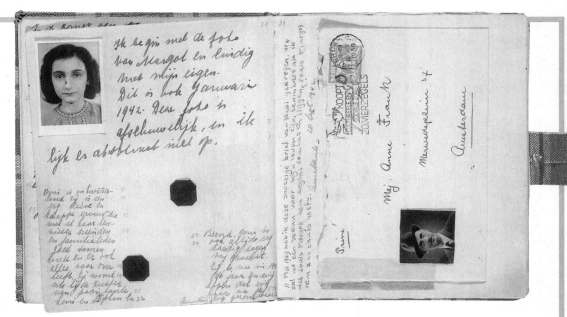

Anne's diary

 Comprehension

A 1 What did Anne call the place in which they were hiding?

    2 What was the name of the family they were sharing this hiding place with?

    3 Why were the Dutch couple 'anxious'?

    4 What happened at two o'clock on the 26th July, 1943?

    5 Why didn't the Frank family try to escape?

B 1 When Anne wrote in her diary on 9th July, 1942, it was her first day in hiding.

    a What kind of mood was she in?

    b What words and phrases could you use to describe her feelings?

    2 When Anne wrote in her diary on 13th January, 1943, she had been hiding for six months.

    a What sort of things was she writing about?

    b How do you think she was feeling?

    3 When Anne wrote in her diary on 26th July, 1943, she had not been outside for a whole year.

    a What sort of things was she writing about?

    b How do you think she was feeling?

C 1 Write a few sentences to explain how you felt after reading the extracts from Anne's diary.

    2 Anne's diary is a first-person account of her experiences. If the events had been written in a third-person account (someone else writing about what had happened to Anne), would you have felt differently? Why?

Vocabulary

Using a thesaurus

Remember, **synonyms** are words or phrases that mean the same, or nearly the same, and **antonyms** are words or phrases that mean the opposite.

Remember, a **thesaurus** can help you to choose the best words to use when you want to describe something or express your feelings. A thesaurus contains lists of words and their **synonyms**, and any **antonyms**. For example:

> **adult** (child) man, woman, grown-up, lady, gentleman, person
> *adulthood*
> **adventure** risk, chance, danger, peril, exploit, hazard
> *adventurous*
> **advice** hint, idea, suggestion, guidance, opinion, wisdom
> *advisable, adviser*
> **advise** (deter) suggest, guide, instruct, persuade, recommend,
> counsel   *advisory*
> **afraid** (bold) scared, frightened, alarmed, worried, nervous,
> terrified

| antonym | word from the same word family | synonyms |

A Use your thesaurus to help you to list the synonyms of each word below. If it has one, write the word's antonym in brackets.

| 1 afraid | 2 stop | 3 brave | 4 angry |
| 5 nasty | 6 alarm | 7 enemy | 8 calm |

B Use your thesaurus to help you make a list of words that you might use to describe each of the situations below. Underline the ones you might select if you were writing about an unpleasant experience.

1 a meal   2 being alone   3 a surprise   4 a journey

Spelling

Adding suffixes

To add a **suffix** when a word ends with 'e', drop the 'e' if the suffix begins with a vowel. For example:

wak<u>e</u> + '<u>i</u>ng' = waking

sham<u>e</u> + '<u>e</u>d' = shamed

Keep the 'e' if the suffix begins with a consonant. For example:

wak<u>e</u> + 'ful' = wak<u>e</u>ful

sham<u>e</u> + 'less' = sham<u>e</u>less

Some exceptions to this rule include:

tru<u>e</u>	truly
argu<u>e</u>	argument
du<u>e</u>	duly

A Add the suffix to each word below and write down the new word that is formed.

1 base + ment

2 care + less

3 state + ment

4 argue + ing

5 combine + ation

6 safe + ty

7 relate + ion

8 package + ing

9 imagine + ation

10 share + ing

11 place + ed

12 insure + ance

B Find and copy the words from the diary entries on pages 4–5 that have suffixes and follow the above rules.

Grammar

'did' and 'done'

Remember, **auxiliary verbs** are words such as 'had', 'have' and 'has'.

There is a useful rule to help you decide when to use '**did**' and when to use '**done**'. We <u>always</u> use an auxiliary (helper) verb when we write 'done' and we <u>never</u> use an auxiliary verb with 'did'. For example:

She had <u>done</u> her best.

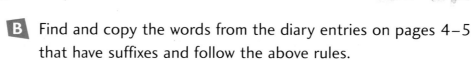

auxiliary verb

She <u>did</u> her best.

A Copy each sentence, choosing the correct verb.

1 *Show them how you did/done it.*

2 *We have did/done this before.*

3 *He showed me what he had did/done.*

4 *Who did/done most of the work?*

5 *When they did/done the last part, it cracked.*

6 *She has did/done it several times.*

7 *I did/done my best to help.*

B Write two sentences, both of which include the words 'did' and 'done', correctly used.

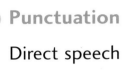

Punctuation

Direct speech

Remember, when you write **direct speech**, you write down the exact words each person said.

Remember, when we write **direct speech**, we use **speech marks** and **commas** to make the meaning clear. For example:
    "Quick! Hide in here," he cried.

A Copy these sentences, adding the missing speech marks and commas.

1 *Have you read Anne Frank's diary? asked my teacher.*

2 *No I replied but I would like to.*

3 *You may borrow my copy if you wish he kindly offered.*

4 *It is a fascinating book he said and an important one, too.*

5 *How could the Nazis be so cruel? I asked.*

6 *That, replied Mr Desai quietly, is something I shall never understand.*

Grace Darling

Information about the life of a real person, written by someone else, is called a biography. This is a short biography of Grace Darling, explaining how and why she became famous.

It was a dark, windy night in 1838. An old Scottish paddle-steamer, the *Forfarshire*, was sailing from Hull to Dundee. Captain Humble knew that one of the ship's boilers was leaking, and we will never know what made him set out on the voyage with his ship in that condition. As a storm began to blow up and the wind and waves grew stronger, both engines suddenly stopped. The ship began drifting helplessly. Knowing that they were in dire trouble, the crew became frightened for their lives.

Captain Humble tried to comfort and encourage everyone, as he had seen a light which he assumed was shining on the island of Inner Farne, off the coast of Northumberland. However, the light was not from Inner Farne but from the Longstone lighthouse, and was there to warn shipping of the treacherous rocks! Suddenly, with a terrifying lurch, the *Forfarshire* struck the Big Hancar rocks. Almost immediately, under the pounding of the raging storm, the vessel began to break up.

By the end of that long and terrible night, only nine survivors, including Captain Humble and his wife, remained clinging to the rocks. Shivering and frightened as the huge waves crashed over them, they knew they could not hold out much longer. At any moment one of the huge waves could drag them into the ferocious sea.

As daybreak came, the lighthouse-keeper's daughter, Grace Darling, woke and looked out from her window. In the distance, she saw shapes on a rock which she thought were seals, which were quite common in those waters. Then, suddenly, as the light became brighter, she realised with horror that they were not seals, but human beings!

The sea was still very rough – far too rough for Grace's father to

row his boat across. It would have been impossible for one person, strong as he was. "But we can't just leave them to drown," pleaded Grace. "If we both go, we can row together."

At first, Mr Darling dismissed the very thought of allowing Grace anywhere near that treacherous sea, but Grace was not to be put off. She couldn't stand by and watch those desperate people swept from the rocks. She was determined that something had to be done. We do not know exactly how Grace persuaded her father, but he eventually agreed that they should go together.

It will never be known how the two felt as they struggled in gale-force winds to launch their small boat into the huge waves, but we do know that the storm was so bad that it nearly sank their flimsy vessel before it reached the rocks. However, once they had started, Grace and Mr Darling knew that they could not abandon their rescue attempt and leave the nine to be swept to their deaths. Straining every muscle, and with little thought for their own survival, they fought and struggled their way through the mountainous waves.

The rowing boat was too small to rescue all nine survivors so, having transferred the first group to the lighthouse, Grace and her father set off again, and were not satisfied until all nine were safely inside the lighthouse.

Grace Darling and her father became national heroes, praised throughout the country for their great bravery, and are remembered to this day for selflessly risking their own lives in order to save others.

Comprehension

A Copy and complete these sentences.

1 The *Forfarshire* was sailing from _____ to _____ .

2 _____ knew that one of the ship's boilers was leaking.

3 The boat struck the _____ rocks.

4 By morning, there were only _____ survivors.

5 The lighthouse keeper was called _____ .

6 Grace knew it was _____ for her father to row out to the rocks alone.

B 1 Do you think the *Forfarshire* should have set out on its voyage? Give reasons for your answer.

2 Why do you think that Mr Darling was reluctant at first to let Grace help him row to the rocks?

3 Explain the following words and phrases.
   a dire trouble   **b** ferocious sea
   c flimsy vessel   **d** selflessly risk their own lives

C The writer is able to tell us many facts about what happened that night but cannot always tell us everything that happened or how people were feeling. Draw a table like the one below.

What we know	What we don't know

Carefully read the passage again and, on your table, write brief notes about:

1 three facts which we can be certain about

2 three things about the incident that are not known for certain.

Vocabulary

Origins of words

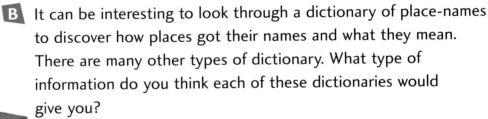

Many words we use today come from words that were used long ago. For example, the suffix 'shire' means a large area of land or a county. Captain Humble's ship, the *Forfarshire*, was named after a region of Scotland.

Many place-names are based on Old English words. For example:

'dun' – hill (e.g. Swin<u>don</u>)

'ingas' – place of (e.g. Hast<u>ings</u>)

'feld' – field (e.g. Maccles<u>field</u>)

A Look at the index of a road map or atlas of Great Britain and try to find three place-names based on each of the old words below. The words sometimes come at the end of the place-name, and sometimes at the beginning.

1 'ceaster' (now 'chester' or 'cester') – an old Roman fortification

2 'ham' – settlement, dwelling-place or homestead

3 'burh' (now often 'burg' or 'burgh') – fort

4 'ford' – river crossing

5 'tun' (now often 'ton') – river crossing

6 'naess' (now 'ness') – headland

7 'cirice' (now 'kirk') – church

B It can be interesting to look through a dictionary of place-names to discover how places got their names and what they mean. There are many other types of dictionary. What type of information do you think each of these dictionaries would give you?

1 dictionary of slang

2 rhyming dictionary

3 etymological dictionary

Spelling

Suffixes 'able' and 'ible'

Many words have the **suffix 'able'** or **'ible'**. For example:

hor<u>rible</u>   depend<u>able</u>

Remember, there is no easy way to decide when to use 'able' and when to use 'ible', but:

- about five times more words end in 'able' than end in 'ible'
- if the antonym of the word is made by adding the prefix 'un', it is probably an 'able' word
- if the antonym of the word is made by adding the prefix 'il', 'in' or 'ir', it is probably an 'ible' word.

For example:

<u>un</u>avail<u>able</u>   <u>in</u>vis<u>ible</u>

A 1 Copy each word, and complete it by adding 'able' or 'ible'.

a *irresist____*   b *unsuit____*

c *incred____*   d *inflex____*

e *unrecognis____*   f *unbeliev____*

2 Complete each word by adding 'able' or 'ible'. It will help if you work out the antonym of each word first.

a *respons____*   b *afford____*

c *bear____*   d *access____*

e *reli____*   f *poss____*

B 1 Write down the words from the box that do not follow the guidelines about antonyms above.

> *inedible   intolerable   insensible   inhospitable*
> *unreasonable   inseparable   indescribable*
> *unfashionable   incurable   incapable   unbreakable*

2 What do you notice about your answer to question 1?

Grammar

Subject and
predicate

Every sentence has a **subject** – the person, place or thing the
sentence is about. The rest of the sentence, including the verb, is called
the **predicate**. For example:

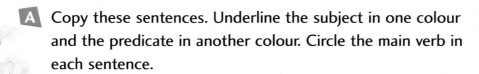

The boiler was leaking.

| subject | predicate |

A Copy these sentences. Underline the subject in one colour
and the predicate in another colour. Circle the main verb in
each sentence.

1 The engines suddenly stopped.

2 Grace looked out of her window.

3 The sea was too rough for Mr Darling to row his boat across.

4 Grace persuaded her father to let her help rescue the people on
the rocks.

5 The lighthouse-keeper's daughter became a national heroine.

B Complete these sentences by adding an interesting predicate to
each subject.

1 The night _____.

2 The Forfarshire _____.

3 Captain Humble _____.

4 A storm _____.

5 Grace Darling _____.

Sentence construction

Connectives and conjunctions

Remember, words and phrases that connect other phrases and clauses in a sentence are called **connectives** or **conjunctions**.

For example:

The captain made a serious error of judgement <u>and, as a result,</u> many lives were lost.

A Copy the sentences below, choosing the most suitable connective from the box to complete each sentence.

> but notwithstanding   and, as a result,   therefore
>
> and, furthermore,   and so inevitably

1 One of the ship's boilers was leaking _____ both engines eventually stopped working.

2 Grace and her father knew the dangers _____ the risks, they set out on their rescue mission.

3 The press published the story _____ Grace and her father became famous.

4 "You can't go alone, _____ I'm coming with you!" insisted Grace.

5 "I'm coming to help you _____ we'll return again and again until all the survivors are safe," she added.

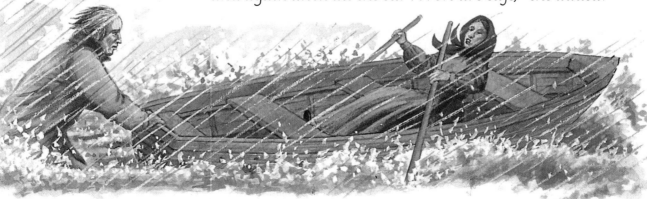

B Use three of the connectives from part A in sentences of your own.

Writing

Biography

A **biography** is written in the third person. A biography can be a whole book about a particular person, or a few facts in a dictionary or encyclopedia. Biographical information may be written as a series of facts about the person but, like the passage about Grace Darling on pages 12–13, some biography is written more descriptively, like a story. Here are some short biographical notes about Grace Darling:

Darling, Grace (1815–42)
- British heroine
- daughter of a lighthouse keeper on the Northumberland coast
- 1838 – helped her father rescue nine survivors from the ship the *Forfarshire*, which had struck the rocks and broken up during a storm

A 1 Choose four people from the list below. Use encyclopedias and reference books to make biographical notes about each of them.

Nelson Mandela	Mother Teresa	Vincent Van Gogh
Florence Nightingale	Mahatma Gandhi	
Beatrix Potter	The Wright Brothers	Marie Curie

2 Use your notes to write a paragraph on each person, saying:
- when and where they lived
- why they are famous.

Autobiography is a person's account of his/her own life or experiences.

If Grace Darling had written an account of that terrible night, we would be able to read it from her point of view. It would have been **autobiographical**.

B Imagine you are Grace Darling and write a first-person account of what happened, starting from the moment you looked out of your window at daybreak and realised that there were people clinging to the rocks. You will need to use your imagination to decide how you think Grace was feeling and what she and her father said to each other.

Victorian Housing

Queen Victoria reigned from 1837 to 1901. In Victorian times, some people were very rich, but huge numbers were extremely poor. During the Victorian period, many people moved from the countryside to the towns, hoping to find work in the new factories that were being built at the time.

Life for the poor

Towns and cities grew larger. To house their new workers, factory owners hastily built rows of small, back-to-back houses, but these were often dark and damp. Sometimes, several families shared one tiny house. The only toilets were outdoor 'earth closets' shared by many people. The smell was foul. Water came from taps in the street or was carried in buckets from nearby wells or rivers. Sewage would often seep into the water supply, which led to the spread of diseases. There were no refuse collections, so the streets were often full of rubbish. The worst streets and alleys were filthy and rat infested. It was very difficult for people to keep themselves and their clothes clean and diseases spread easily. Poor nutrition and illness meant that many people did not live beyond childhood.

Eventually, some factory owners realised that their workers would do a better job if they were healthy, had comfortable homes and were well fed. Robert Owen built some bigger and better homes for his workers at New Lanark, and William and James Lever, the soapmakers, created a new 'industrial village' at Port Sunlight, near Warrington. But, for most of the workers and their families, life was very hard.

Inside the house of a working family.

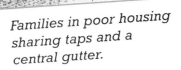

Families in poor housing sharing taps and a central gutter.

A street of grand houses in London.

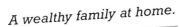

A wealthy family at home.

Life for the rich

The houses of people such as doctors, factory managers and government officials were very different from the 'back-to-backs'. They often had beautiful gardens and were in pleasant, wide streets. They usually had spacious rooms on several floors, with expensive, comfortable furniture. The walls were hung with pictures in heavy frames and the curtains were of satin and lace. These houses had toilets.

Wealthy people could afford to employ servants to live in the house and do the cleaning and laundry and prepare meals. Servants usually slept in small rooms at the top of the house. They worked very long hours, but at least they were usually warm and well fed.

Homes at the industrial village of Port Sunlight, built by the Lever brothers.

 Comprehension **A**

1. For how long did Queen Victoria reign?
2. Why did many people move from the country to the towns during the Victorian period?
3. Why was there so much disease among the poor?
4. Robert Owen and the Lever brothers built better homes for their workers. Why was this?
5. Make notes on the differences between the houses of the very poor and those of the rich.

B Write a paragraph to explain what you would find most difficult if you had to travel back in time and live in the house of a poor person in Victorian times.

C
1. The writer has used two sub-headings to organise the report. How are the two sections different?
2. How many paragraphs are there in the report?
3. Summarise in a few words the content of each paragraph.
4. Why do you think the writer has included photographs?

Vocabulary

Eponyms

Remember, an **eponym** is a word that is based on a person's name.
For example:

Victorian – after Queen Victoria

the sandwich – after the fourth Earl of Sandwich

A Write down what each of the people gave their name to. Use a dictionary or encyclopaedia to help you if you cannot guess.

1 Mrs A. Bloomer
2 Joseph Ignace Guillotin
3 Samuel Plimsoll
4 Laszlo Biro

B Choose four words from the box below. Use dictionaries, encyclopaedias and other reference material to research the origin of each word.

> **bobby** – the slang name for a police officer
> **pasteurisation** – the process of making milk safe to drink
> **America** – the continent
> **Celsius** – a measurement of temperature
> **the Carroll diagram** – a mathematical diagram
> **the pavlova** – a type of dessert
> **Marxism** – a political belief
> **tarmac** – the surface on most roads

Remember, to make a **noun plural** we normally add 's'. For example:
    teacher   teacher<u>s</u>

But if the noun ends with 's', 'x', 'ch' or 'sh', we add 'es'. For example:
    gas   ga<u>ses</u>   fox   fox<u>es</u>
    church   church<u>es</u>   brush   brush<u>es</u>

If a noun ends in 'y', we usually change the 'y' to 'i' and add 'es'.
For example:
    countr<u>y</u>   countr<u>ies</u>

But if the letter before the 'y' is a vowel, simply add 's'. For example:
    day   days

A Write the plural of each of these words.

1 berry	2 star	3 watch	4 activity
5 dish	6 alley	7 pony	8 horse
9 difficulty	10 box	11 valley	12 quay
13 company	14 fly	15 torch	16 bus
17 sound	18 father	19 moon	20 marsh

Remember, when a **verb** goes with a <u>singular</u> noun, we often add 's' or 'es', and the rules are the same as for nouns. For example:

	Plural	Singular
+ 's':	they talk	he talks
+ 'es':	they fix	he fixes
	they pass	he passes
	they catch	he catches
	they push	he pushes
change 'y' to 'i' and add 'es':	they cry	he cries

B Write down four more verbs that change in each of the following ways to go with a singular noun.

    1 + 's'   2 + 'es'   3 change 'y' to 'i' and add 'es'

Grammar

Complex sentences

Remember, a **simple sentence** is made up of one main clause.

A **compound sentence** is made up of two or more simple sentences joined by a conjunction. For example:

Simple sentence: Thousands of houses were built to house the workers.

Simple sentence: They were not very well designed.

Compound sentence: <u>Thousands of houses were built to house the workers</u> but <u>they were not very well designed</u>.

A **complex sentence** is made up of one **main clause** and one or more other clauses – called **subordinate clauses**. Subordinate clauses cannot make sense on their own. For example:

<u>Thousands of houses were built</u> to house the new workers.

| main clause | subordinate clause |

A Copy these complex sentences and underline the main clause in each.

1 Many of the houses were cold and damp, causing sickness and disease to be common and widespread.

2 Sewage would sometimes leak into the water supply, leading to the spread of serious diseases.

3 Some factory owners built better houses, believing that good housing was essential for a productive workforce.

Be careful! Make a **complex sentence**, not a compound sentence.

B Add a subordinate clause to each sentence to make it more interesting and informative.

1 Samuel's father moved the family to Bradford.

2 His father worked in the cotton mill.

3 Samuel worked hard at his lessons.

Sentence construction

Complex sentences

In the Grammar section of this unit, you learned that a **complex sentence** is made up of one main clause, and one or more other clauses, called **subordinate clauses**, which do not make sense on their own.

In a complex sentence, the main clause is not necessarily the first clause. For example:

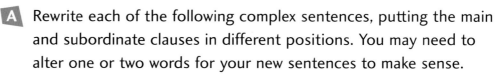

To fetch water for drinking, many people had to walk to the nearest pump or river.

| subordinate clause | main clause |

As a result of disease, often caused by dirty water, many Victorian children died.

| subordinate clause | subordinate clause | main clause |

A Rewrite each of the following complex sentences, putting the main and subordinate clauses in different positions. You may need to alter one or two words for your new sentences to make sense.

1 *For most workers in Victorian times, life was hard.*

2 *Some Victorians had very comfortable lives, while others lived in terrible poverty.*

3 *Before the invention of machines, which could do the work of many people, there were no factories.*

B Copy each sentence twice, each time adding the same subordinate clause but in a different place. The first has been done to help you.

1 *Rich people often lit their houses by gaslight.*

   Rich people often lit their houses by gaslight, which gave a better light than candles.

   As it gave a better light than candles, rich people often lit their houses by gaslight.

2 *The Lever brothers created a new village at Port Sunlight.*

3 *Servants' bedrooms were usually at the top of the house.*

4 *Many workers moved into the cities.*

Writing

Reports

A **report** is a piece of non-fiction information text. It must:

- have an introduction, telling the reader what the report is about; this could just be a short paragraph
- be organised into paragraphs and divided into sections with sub-headings
- give factual information
- give the information in a sensible order.

To write a report, you need to:

- Research – use sources of information to find the facts you need for your report. Remember to keep a list of the sources for your bibliography.
- Make notes – your notes should be short and in your own words. You may copy out phrases and sentences if you want to quote them in your report, but remember to acknowledge your sources.
- Include illustrations, such as diagrams or photographs – these are a good way of providing information.
- Write a first draft – then check it carefully.
- Neatly copy your report and add a bibliography.

A Imagine you are an Inspector of Housing in Victorian times. Your job is to write a report about the housing of the poor. The aim of your report is to persuade other factory owners to follow the example of Robert Owen and the Lever brothers and build better houses for their workers.

Many of the facts you need are on pages 20–21, but you should use other reference books to find out as much as you can about housing for poorer people during the Victorian period.

B Choose one of the following subjects, research it, make notes and then write a report about it.

- Victorian clothing
- Victorian food
- Victorian transport
- Victorian schools

The Hostile Desert

Deserts can be hostile and dangerous places, especially for those who are unfamiliar with them. Here is an extract from a fictional description of a journey across part of the Sahara Desert, which is written in an autobiographical style.

As we left they told us the old joke. "To start a journey in a sandstorm is good luck."

We camped the first night twenty miles south. The next morning we woke and came out of our tents at five. Too cold to sleep … Above us were the last stars. There would be no sunrise for another two hours. We passed around hot glasses of tea. The camels were being fed, half asleep, chewing the dates along with the date stones. We ate breakfast and then drank three more glasses of tea.

Hours later we were in the sandstorm that hit us out of a clear morning, coming from nowhere. The breeze that had been refreshing had gradually strengthened. Eventually we looked down, and the surface of the desert was changed. Pass me the book … here. This is Hassanein Bey's wonderful account of such storms –

It is as though the surface were underlaid with steam-pipes, with thousands of orifices through which tiny jets of steam are puffing out. The sand leaps in little spurts and whirls. Inch by inch the disturbance rises as the wind increases its force. It seems as though the whole surface of the desert were rising in obedience to some upthrusting force beneath. Larger pebbles strike against the shins, the knees, the thighs. The sand-grains climb the body till it strikes the face and goes over the head. The sky is shut out, all but the nearest objects fade from view, the universe is filled.

We had to keep moving. If you pause sand builds up as it would around anything stationary, and locks you in. You are lost forever. A sandstorm can last five hours. Even when we were in trucks in later years we would have to keep driving with no vision.

The worst terrors came at night. Once, north of Kufra, we were hit by a storm in the darkness. Three a.m. The gale swept the tents from their moorings and we rolled with them, taking in sand like a sinking boat takes in water, weighed down, suffocating, till we were cut free by a camel driver.

We travelled through three storms during nine days. We missed small desert towns where we expected to locate more supplies. The horse vanished. Three camels died. For the last two days there was no food, only tea ... After the third night we gave up talking. All that mattered was the fire and the minimal brown liquid.

Only by luck did we stumble on the desert town of El Taj.

from *The English Patient* by Michael Ondaatje

Comprehension

A Copy and complete each sentence, using one or more words.

1 They travelled a distance of _____ on the first day.

2 _____ was their main drink throughout the journey.

3 In a sandstorm it is important to _____.

4 During the journey, _____ died.

5 They travelled through _____ storms in _____ days.

B Write sentences to answer each question.

1 In which desert were they travelling?

2 The writer quotes Hassanein Bey's account of a sandstorm. What do you think Bey means by 'the universe is filled'?

3 Why do you think the travellers were particularly concerned about the nights?

4 What similarity does the writer suggest between being in a desert and being at sea. Can you think of any others?

5 Why do you think the travellers 'gave up talking' after the third night?

C Carefully read Hassanein Bey's account of what it is like being in a sandstorm. You have probably never experienced a sandstorm but did his account give you a good idea of what one must be like? Write a few sentences to explain whether you think his description is a good one, giving your reasons.

Vocabulary

Hyperbole

Hyperbole often involves the use of common **idioms**.

'**Hyperbole**' means exaggeration. For example, it would be hyperbole to say:

   I was so thirsty I could have drunk the river dry.

It can be fun to use hyperbole occasionally, but it really weakens your argument if you want your reader to take you seriously.

A Rewrite these statements so that they are less exaggerated.

1   My clothes were so dirty they could have stood up on their own.

2   It was so cold, I thought I would freeze to death.

3   You could have knocked me down with a feather.

4   I didn't close my eyes all night.

B Copy each example of hyperbole, below, matching it with a less exaggerated phrase from the box.

felt angry	felt tired	is untidy
feel hungry	fell over	is confused

1   couldn't keep my eyes open

2   looks like a bomb's hit it

3   doesn't know what day of the week it is

4   saw red

5   went head over heels

6   could eat a horse

31

Spelling

Suffixes 'ous' and 'ious'

Here are two groups of words that often cause problems, even for good spellers. You simply need to learn and remember which words end with the **suffix 'ous'** and which end with **'ious'**.

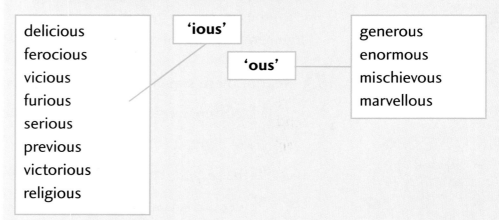

'ious'	'ous'
delicious	generous
ferocious	enormous
vicious	mischievous
furious	marvellous
serious	
previous	
victorious	
religious	

A 1 Cover the box above, then write one word to go with each of these clues. Each answer must end with 'ous' or 'ious'.

a tasty
b very angry
c huge
d winning
e frighteningly aggressive
f wonderful
g solemn
h having a religion

2 Use each of the following words in a sentence of your own.

a *mischievous*
b *generous*
c *previous*
d *marvellous*

To add the suffix 'ous' or 'ious' to most words ending with 'our', drop the 'u' in the root word. For example:
vapo̲u̲r + 'ous' = vaporous

B Copy each of the following words and draw a circle around the letter you must drop. Then, add 'ous' or 'ious'. The first one has been done to help you.

1 *humour*   humo(u)r + ous = humorous
2 *labour*
3 *glamour*
4 *rigour*
5 *vigour*

Grammar

Noun and verb agreement

Remember, when we say that the **nouns** and **verbs** in a sentence must **agree**, we mean that, in a sentence, the nouns and verbs must 'match', depending on whether the noun is singular or plural. For example:

The camel <u>eats</u> dates.
The camels <u>eat</u> the dates.
You <u>are</u> very kind.
They <u>were</u> very kind.

A Copy and complete these sentences, adding 'is', 'are', 'was' or 'were' in each gap. Read all the sentences before starting.

1 We _____ going on a journey.

2 It _____ a dangerous trip.

3 You _____ welcome to join us.

4 We _____ planning to go last month.

5 The weather _____ not good enough, so we had to wait.

6 I _____ very disappointed.

7 We _____ well prepared for the trip.

8 It _____ very cold at night in the desert.

B Copy these sentences, choosing the correct verb to complete each one.

1 I like/likes travelling.

2 We have/has packed all our equipment.

3 We ride/rides at night, before the heat becomes unbearable.

4 I go/goes to check my camel.

5 He never hurt/hurts anyone.

6 I give/gives him as much water as he wants.

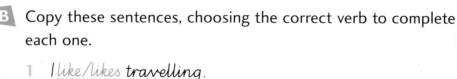

33

Remember, a **clause** is a group of words in a sentence that has its own verb. For example, this sentence has two clauses, joined by a **conjunction**:

The sun was hot so we wore our hats.

| main clause | conjunction | subordinate clause |

A Copy each sentence and underline each clause in a different colour. Draw a ring around the conjunction.

1 I can now ride a camel well, although it makes me feel seasick!

2 The worst time was at night when the cold winds blew.

3 We had excellent guides who knew all the dangers.

4 We were going on a long journey so we took a good supply of food and water.

Remember, in a **complex sentence**, the **main clause** makes sense by itself; the others are **subordinate clauses**.

B 1 Use conjunctions from the box to add two different subordinate clauses to each of the main clauses below, making sentences. The first one has been done to help you.

| and | so | although | because | after | before | when | but |

a The camels were powerful

The camels were powerful and able to carry heavy loads.

The camels were powerful although their legs looked thin and fragile.

b Deserts are dangerous places

c I wasn't frightened

d We eventually reached El Taj

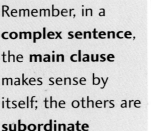

Remember, the main clause of a complex sentence does not have to come first.

2 Copy these sentences and underline the main clause in each.

a *As soon as I put my head down I was fast asleep.*

b *Sand had got into everything by the time we completed our journey.*

c *Whilst exploring them is exciting, deserts can be extremely dangerous.*

d *Although we warned them against it, they set off despite the sandstorm forecast.*

Writing

Autobiographies

Remember, **autobiography** is someone's written account of his/her experiences. In the passage on pages 28–29, the writer has imagined himself to have travelled across the Sahara Desert. He has written his story in the first person, using an autobiographical style.

A Make notes about a journey that you have been on. This could be:
- your journey to school
- going on holiday
- a visit to a friend or relation
- travelling to live in a new area.

Use your notes to write an autobiographical account of your journey, so your reader can imagine exactly what it was like and how you felt. Remember, when writing in the first person, avoid beginning every sentence with 'I', by:
- changing the order of the words in some sentences
- joining pairs of shorter sentences with a conjunction.

B Imagine that you are a traveller in some exotic place. This could be:
- the Himalayas • the Amazon rainforest • the Antarctic
or you may have your own ideas.

1 Use reference books to research the place you have chosen.
2 Make notes on the climate, landscape, etc.
3 Use your notes to write an account of your journey in an autobiographical style so the reader can imagine exactly what it was like and how you felt.

The Great Dinosaur Mystery

Dinosaurs first walked the Earth over 200 million years ago. The word 'dinosaur', first used by zoologist Richard Owen in 1841, comes from the Greek, meaning 'terrible lizard'. The dinosaurs were reptiles but, in fact, they were not true lizards. There were many different types of dinosaur, from the gigantic to the tiny; some lived in the oceans, others were able to fly but most lived on the land. The majority were herbivores but a few were deadly predators. The dinosaurs were such a successful species that, for 150 million years, they dominated the Earth.

Scientists have always been fascinated by dinosaurs, but one of the most interesting things about them is the mystery of why, 65 million years ago, the dinosaurs suddenly died out and disappeared from the Earth forever. Scientists have come up with several theories:

- that certain smaller animals took to eating dinosaurs' eggs
- that a nearby exploding star showered the Earth with deadly x-rays
- that the climate gently changed, causing the sea level to rise, which destroyed the dinosaurs' habitats
- that one or more huge meteors from space collided with the Earth, causing dramatic climate change.

Let's examine each theory in order:

Destruction of eggs
This theory is very difficult to prove. Most creatures will defend their eggs and their young against anything, even if it means being killed themselves. It seems highly unlikely that all the different types of dinosaur should have had this problem at about the same time.

Deadly x-rays
The universe contains many mysteries, and the possibility of deadly radioactive x-rays reaching Earth from an exploding star is an interesting notion. Such radioactivity is not apparent in rocks that contain fossilised dinosaur remains, but it might have been there once and gradually dispersed over the millions of intervening years. Unfortunately, there is no way to prove or disprove this theory.

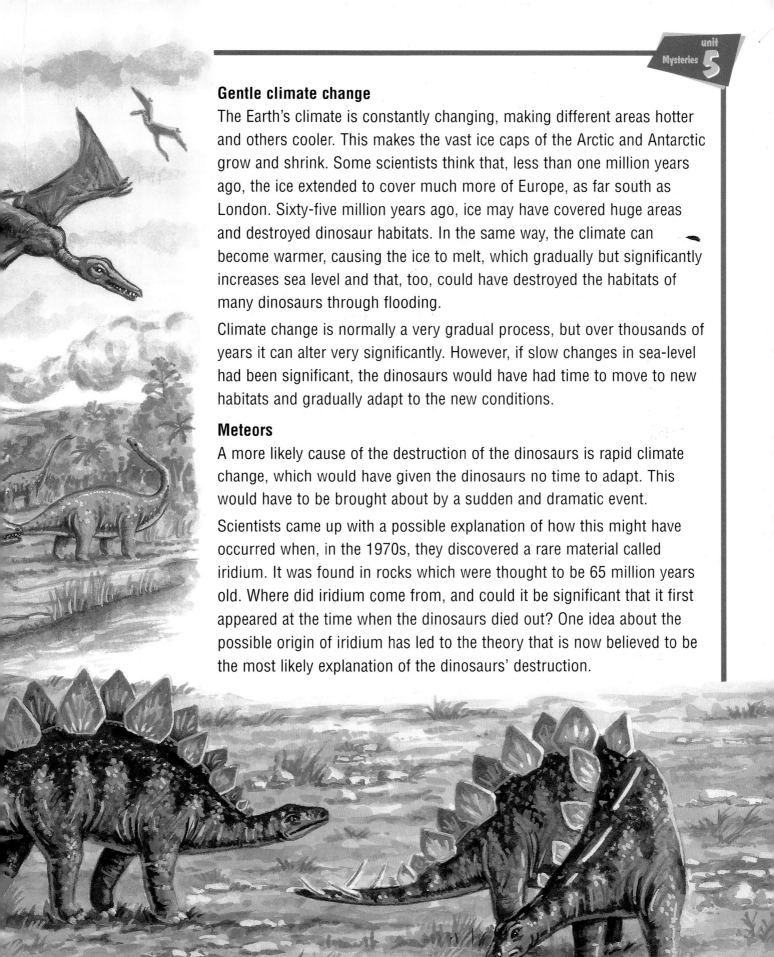

Gentle climate change

The Earth's climate is constantly changing, making different areas hotter and others cooler. This makes the vast ice caps of the Arctic and Antarctic grow and shrink. Some scientists think that, less than one million years ago, the ice extended to cover much more of Europe, as far south as London. Sixty-five million years ago, ice may have covered huge areas and destroyed dinosaur habitats. In the same way, the climate can become warmer, causing the ice to melt, which gradually but significantly increases sea level and that, too, could have destroyed the habitats of many dinosaurs through flooding.

Climate change is normally a very gradual process, but over thousands of years it can alter very significantly. However, if slow changes in sea-level had been significant, the dinosaurs would have had time to move to new habitats and gradually adapt to the new conditions.

Meteors

A more likely cause of the destruction of the dinosaurs is rapid climate change, which would have given the dinosaurs no time to adapt. This would have to be brought about by a sudden and dramatic event.

Scientists came up with a possible explanation of how this might have occurred when, in the 1970s, they discovered a rare material called iridium. It was found in rocks which were thought to be 65 million years old. Where did iridium come from, and could it be significant that it first appeared at the time when the dinosaurs died out? One idea about the possible origin of iridium has led to the theory that is now believed to be the most likely explanation of the dinosaurs' destruction.

It is believed that the iridium may have come from outer space, and that it probably arrived as part of one or more huge meteors which collided with Earth. In the 65 million years since they were formed, the craters caused by these meteors were worn away, but evidence of more recent collisions with meteorites can still be seen today.

But how could something striking the Earth 65 million years ago have killed all the dinosaurs? The theory is that, if the meteor had been big enough, the impact would have created enormous amounts of rock and dust. This would have been thrown up into the Earth's atmosphere and spread around the world, blocking out most of the Sun's rays. For months, or even years, the climate would have been dramatically different. There would have been little light or heat and the Earth would have been permanently cold, frosty and dark. Plants would have died and the animals which lived on those plants would have starved, including the dinosaurs. Small animals might have been able to survive by nibbling bark or seeds, or even the frozen bodies of larger animals but, by the time the skies had cleared, letting in warmth and light from the Sun, it would have been too late for the dinosaurs.

Comprehension A

1 What does 'dinosaur' mean?
2 How long ago did the dinosaurs die out?
3 What were the two possible effects of slow climate change on the dinosaurs' habitats?
4 Where do scientists believe iridium came from?

Use your dictionary if you need to.

B 1 Write down what you understand by each of the following terms from the passage.

a herbivores	b predators	c habitats
d gradually dispersed	e intervening years	f meteors
g impact	h collided	i craters

2 How do you think the scientists knew that iridium had first appeared at about the time the dinosaurs died out?

C Of the theories about why the dinosaurs died out, which do you think most likely to be true? Give reasons for your choice and explain why you are less sure about the other theories.

Vocabulary

Using a thesaurus

Remember, when you are writing, a thesaurus can help you to find the best words to express what you want to say. A **thesaurus** provides a selection of synonyms – words that mean the same, or are very similar – for the word you have looked up. For example:

> **terrible**   awful, shocking, frightful, horrible, gruesome, horrendous

A List the words in your thesaurus that appear under these headings.

1	afraid	2	grab	3	harm
4	prevent	5	destroy	6	mistake

B Write some sentences of your own about dinosaurs. In each sentence, use one of the synonyms you wrote down in part A.

Spelling

'ie' or 'ei'?

It is helpful to remember that 'i' comes before 'e' when the sound is 'ee'. For example:

p<u>ie</u>ce   rel<u>ie</u>ve

But 'i' does not come before 'e' when it follows a 'c'. For example:

rec<u>ei</u>ve   c<u>ei</u>ling

And 'i' does not come before 'e' when the sound is not 'ee'. For example:

r<u>ei</u>gn   v<u>ei</u>l

A Sort the words from the box into three lists:

'ei' because the	**'ei' because it**	**'ie' because the**
sound isn't 'ee':	**follows 'c':**	**sound is 'ee':**

Write each word from the box under the correct heading.

> their   deceive   neither   receipt   eight
>
> field   sovereign   believe   conceit   wield   brief
>
> weigh   rein   chief   reindeer   shield   vein
>
> leisure   achieve   heir   relief   foreign   forfeit
>
> priest   retrieve   deceit

If you are stuck, think of some words from the same word families as those in part A.

B Write down two more words which have the same spelling pattern as:

1 'piece' ('ie' in a word with an 'ee' sound)
2 'receive' ('ei' after a 'c')
3 'reign' ('ei' in a word that doesn't have an 'ee' sound)

 Grammar

Active and passive sentences

Remember, if the action of the verb is done by the subject of the sentence, we call it an **active verb** and an **active sentence**. For example:

The scientist studied the dinosaur's skeleton.

subject	verb

If the subject of the sentence has the action of the verb done to it, then we call it a **passive verb** and a **passive sentence**. For example:

The dinosaur's skeleton was studied by the scientist.

subject	verb

A 1 Copy each sentence. Underline the subject in one colour and the verb in another. Write whether each sentence is active or passive.

a The Earth was dominated by some of the most extraordinary creatures.

b Richard Owen devised the name 'dinosaur'.

c The Earth's climate has been affected by human pollution.

d Some huge, ancient craters were caused by meteorites.

e Vast quantities of dust cut out the Sun's rays.

2 Look at the passive sentences from question 1. What two things do they have in common?

unit
Mysteries **5**

B 1 Look back at question 1 in part A.

    a   Rewrite the passive sentences as active.

    b   Rewrite the active sentences as passive.

  2 a   Write a sentence to say what you had to do to change the passive sentences to active.

    b   Write a sentence to say what you had to do to change the active sentences to passive.

Sentence construction

Expanding sentences

Sentences can often be **expanded**, to make them more interesting or clearer, by adding words, phrases or clauses. For example:

    The dinosaur ate the leaves.

    The <u>enormous</u> dinosaur <u>extended its giraffe-like neck and contentedly</u> ate the <u>succulent green</u> leaves.

When looking at a sentence that you have written, ask yourself whether you need to add more detail to answer the following questions:

What kind?	When?	How?	Which?
Where?	How often?	How much?	How many?

Words that will be particularly useful for answering these questions are:

- **adjectives** – words that tell us more about nouns
- **adverbs** – words that tell us how, when or where the action of a verb takes place
- **prepositions** – words that tell us the position of something.

A Expand each of these sentences to answer the questions in brackets.

1 *A dinosaur was sleeping.* (What kind? Where? How?)

2 *It opened its eyes.* (Why? How?)

3 *It saw another dinosaur coming.* (Where? What kind? How?)

4 *It stood up.* (How? Why?)

5 *There was a fight.* (When? What kind?)

6 *The dinosaur went back to sleep.* (When? Where? How much?)

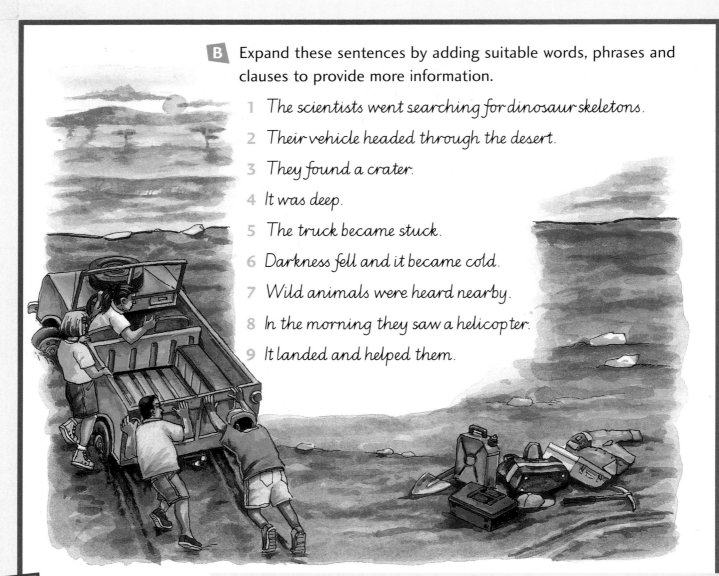

B Expand these sentences by adding suitable words, phrases and clauses to provide more information.

1 The scientists went searching for dinosaur skeletons.

2 Their vehicle headed through the desert.

3 They found a crater.

4 It was deep.

5 The truck became stuck.

6 Darkness fell and it became cold.

7 Wild animals were heard nearby.

8 In the morning they saw a helicopter.

9 It landed and helped them.

Writing

Constructing an argument

Some types of non-fiction writing present an **argument** – a case for or against something. This sort of writing needs to include facts and opinions. A balanced argument will investigate the main ideas, and then come to a conclusion.

In 'The Great Dinosaur Mystery', the writer looks at all the possible theories about why the dinosaurs died out, then comes to a conclusion about which is the most likely.

A Carefully read 'The Great Dinosaur Mystery' again. Write these headings in your book:

Theory	True or False?

1 Under the heading 'Theory', make brief notes on all the possible reasons why the dinosaurs died out.
2 Under the heading 'True or false?', make notes on why each theory is likely to be true or is probably false.

B Choose one of the following:

• Is there life on other planets?

• Should children be allowed to watch whatever they like on television?

• Do ghosts exist?

• Should children be allowed to go to bed whenever they like?

Make notes on both sides of the argument. You could ask other people what they think. Use your notes to construct a balanced argument which includes:

• a paragraph for each different opinion or idea
• a paragraph to explain why you believe each opinion or idea is right or wrong
• a paragraph at the end, giving your conclusion.

Unidentified flying objects exist. Of that there is absolutely no doubt. They have been seen, photographed and filmed by astronauts, airline pilots, police officers, astronomers, meteorologists and farmers. The big mystery, that has remained unsolved since the popular term 'flying saucer' was first coined in 1947, is: 'What are they and where do they come from?'

All kinds of explanations have been put forward to account for the worldwide sightings of discs, egg shapes, spheres and other oddly shaped aerial objects. They have been explained away as unusual cloud formations, fireballs, meteorites, weather balloons, optical illusions, hallucinations or simply fabrications engineered by publicity-seeking cranks.

But not every reported case can be dismissed in this way. The most logical attitude towards UFOs is that we are faced with a series of inexplicable, but nonetheless real, phenomena.

The attitude of ufologists – students of UFOs – goes a step further. They usually claim that the earth is under surveillance by alien intelligences.

Tomorrow, perhaps, the truth will emerge. Meanwhile, humankind is left with a puzzling mass of evidence that ranges from impartial, level-headed accounts to the totally implausible ... Is earth being watched by beings from another planet? If so, what is the purpose of these aliens?

Humans, it seems, will simply have to wait until the extra-terrestrials make themselves properly known to learn the answers to these and other questions. Either that or find another explanation for the strange objects seen over and on the earth.

The first flying saucers

The flying saucer story began on June 24, 1947, when a private pilot, Kenneth Arnold, who was taking part in a search for a missing transport aircraft, saw nine disc-shaped objects flying over Mount Rainier, Washington, USA. He described the objects as 'flying like a saucer would if you skimmed it across the water' ... His account of the incident was accepted by the authorities. Newspapers picked up the story and labelled the objects 'flying saucers'.

Astronauts sight UFOs!

It is not only people on Earth or in aeroplanes who have seen UFOs. Since the 1960s, many astronauts have reported seeing UFOs.

United States astronaut, James McDivitt, claimed to have seen a UFO in June 1965. In orbit, about 90 miles (145 km) above the Earth, McDivitt saw a cylindrical object, apparently with arms sticking out of it, which he took to be another spacecraft with antennae.

... McDivitt took one still photograph and some film. He observed that the object was moving in a parallel path to his own spacecraft, but closing in fast. McDivitt and his fellow-astronaut, Edward White, were hastily preparing to take evasive action when the UFO disappeared from view.

... Originally, McDivitt thought he had seen some un-staffed satellite. The official view was that he had spotted the ... US satellite *Pegasus*. But that was 1,200 miles (1,932 km) away at the time of his sighting. Captain Ed Mitchell, the sixth man to walk on the moon, told a press conference in 1974: 'I am completely convinced that *some* UFO sightings are real. The question isn't where the UFOs are from. The question is what they are.'

Comprehension

A

1 When was the term 'flying saucer' first used?
2 List three of the other possible explanations for flying saucers that are mentioned.
3 What are people who study UFOs called?
4 Why was it unlikely that what McDivitt saw was the US satellite *Pegasus*?
5 Who was completely convinced that some UFO sightings were real?

B

1 Explain the following words and phrases.
   a aerial objects
   b hallucinations
   c under surveillance
   d extra-terrestrials
   e evasive action
2 Do you think the person who wrote the passage believes in UFOs? Give your reasons.

C Carefully read the passage again. Write a few sentences to explain whether it convinces you that UFOs exist.

Vocabulary

Proverbs

A **proverb** is a wise saying that contains a general truth. Many are centuries old. Most countries have their own proverbs, and some are very similar from country to country. For example:

Great minds think alike.

This proverb would be said by people who agree with each other, believing that if they agree they must be right. (But, of course, they could both be wrong!)

A 1 Write in your own words the meaning of each of these proverbs.

 a The early bird catches the worm.

 b A fool and his money are soon parted.

 c Two wrongs don't make a right.

 2 Now use each proverb from question 1 in a sentence or short piece of dialogue.

B 1 Match each of the proverb beginnings below with the correct ending from the box. Write out each proverb in full.

a Empty vessels	without fire
b More haste	are better than one
c A stitch in time	the mice will play
d While the cat's away	less speed
e Two heads	make the most sound
f Birds of a feather	saves nine
g There's no smoke	flock together

 2 Write the meaning of each proverb you completed in question 1.

Spelling

Adding 'll' prefixes and suffixes

To add a **prefix** ending with 'll' to a word, we usually drop one 'l' from the prefix. For example:

'al̲l' + ways = al̲ways

To add a **suffix** ending with 'll' to many words, we drop one 'l' from the suffix. For example:

doubt + 'ful̲l' = doubtful̲

If the word also ends with 'll', we sometimes delete one 'l' from the word, as well as one from the suffix. For example:

wil̲l + 'ful̲l' = wil̲ful̲

However, this is not a rule, as there are several exceptions, especially words with a 'ness' suffix. For example:

still + 'ness' = stil̲lness

A Add the prefix or suffix to each word below. Check your answers in a dictionary. Some are exceptions to the rule!

a	joy + full	b	all + most
c	all + mighty	d	full + ness
e	full + fill	f	all + so
g	shrill + ness	h	skill + full
i	care + full	j	all + together
k	all + though	l	fate + full
m	hill + side	n	spoon + full

B Look in your dictionary and list the words that begin with the sound 'all' (as in 'ball') but only have a single 'l', such as 'always'.

Grammar

'Helper' verbs

Remember, it is sometimes difficult to know when to use **'helper' verbs**, or auxiliary verbs. Never use a 'helper' verb with:

froze	chose	spoke	broke

Always use a 'helper' verb with:

frozen	chosen	spoken	broken

For example:

I <u>chose</u> to read a book about UFOs.

I <u>have chosen</u> to read a book about UFOs.

A Copy these sentences, choosing the correct verb to complete each one.

1 It was very cold this morning, and the bird bath was <u>froze/frozen</u>.

2 I <u>broke/broken</u> the ice so the birds could have a drink.

3 We all <u>chose/chosen</u> hot porridge for breakfast.

4 Mum rushed in, saying that our water pipes were <u>froze/frozen</u>.

5 Dad asked if she had <u>spoke/spoken</u> to the plumber.

6 Mum told him that the telephone had <u>broke/broken</u>.

7 Mum was in a bad mood, so Dad <u>chose/chosen</u> to keep out of her way!

Other verbs that need a 'helper' verb are:

known	grown	thrown

B Put each word into a sentence of your own. Remember to use a 'helper' verb with verbs that need one.

1 know   2 known   3 grow

4 grown   5 throw   6 thrown

Colons and semi-colons

Remember, **colons** are sometimes used at the beginning of a list. For example:

> I am inviting to my party: Bharti, Jeremy, Sunil, Rees, Harry, Layla and Sue.
>
> For this recipe you will need: flour, eggs, sugar, butter, cocoa powder, chopped nuts.

Semi-colons are used between the clauses in a compound sentence instead of a conjunction. For example:

> UFOs definitely exist; there are certainly many people who believe it.

A Copy these sentences, adding the missing colons and other punctuation marks.

1. In our class, the following people believe in UFOs Kenneth Ross Louisa Edwards Ellen Davies Bryan Finn and Clara Leigh

2. UFOs have been described in many ways including discs egg shapes spheres flying cigars and frisbees

3. Possible explanations for UFOs are cloud formations fireballs meteorites weather balloons optical illusions hallucinations

B Copy these sentences, adding the missing semi-colons and other punctuation marks.

1. I sometimes go on UFO-spotting trips with my brother Dad comes too if he isn't working

2. On some nights there are crowds of people on the hillside looking for flying saucers only the real enthusiasts come when its frosty

3. Last night we started off looking for UFOs we ended up watching a nest of owls

4. By midnight it was getting cold we decided to go home

Writing

Convincing your audience

The writer of the passage on UFOs obviously believes that such things exist and tries to **convince** the reader by:

- listing the various sorts of people who have seen UFOs
- listing the other things that UFOs could be, but says that not all UFO sightings can be explained in this way
- showing how improbable it is that McDivitt's sighting was a satellite
- quoting Captain Ed Mitchell's opinion to support the argument.

In Unit 5 of this book, you were asked to choose one of the following subjects and write a <u>balanced</u> argument.

- Is there life on other planets?
- Should children have to go to school?
- Do ghosts exist?
- Should children be allowed to go to bed whenever they like?

Now, choose one of the three you did not write about in Unit 5. Decide which side of the argument you are on:

• There is life on other planets	or	• Life does not exist on other planets
• Children should be allowed to watch whatever they like on television	or	• Children should not be allowed to watch whatever they like on television
• Ghosts do exist	or	• There are no such things as ghosts
• Children should be allowed to go to bed whenever they like	or	• Children should go to bed when adults tell them to

Write a report which supports your side of the argument. Include evidence that supports the opposite view, and provide information that proves it wrong. Think about the sort of things somebody with the opposing view might say, and try to find ways of arguing against their points.

The Hairy Hands

One day in June, 1921, Doctor E.M. Helby, Medical Officer to the prison at Princetown, was riding on his motor-bicycle along the road which crosses Dartmoor from Two Bridges to Moretonhampstead.

In the sidecar attached to the machine there were two children. They were travelling down the slope towards the bridge which crosses the East Dart near Postbridge, when, according to the account given by the children afterwards, the doctor suddenly shouted out, "There's something wrong. Jump!"

The next moment the bicycle swerved, the engine broke away from its fastenings and the doctor was hurled from his seat into the roadway. He landed on his head with such force that he was killed instantly. Luckily, the two children were unhurt.

On August 26, 1921, a young officer left the house of a friend on a motor-bicycle, with the intention of visiting some people at a considerable distance. An hour later he returned to his friend's house, cut and bruised, his bicycle badly damaged. While he was having his hurts tended, his friend asked him to describe how the accident had happened. A queer look came into the young man's eyes and he said: "You will find it difficult to believe, but something drove me off the road. A pair of hairy hands closed over mine – I felt them as plainly as ever I felt anything in my life – large, muscular hairy hands. I fought against them as hard as I could, but it was no use, they were too strong for me. They forced the machine into the side of the road, and I knew no more until I came to my senses, lying on my face on the turf a few feet away from the bicycle."

The spot where the accident occurred was close to the place where Dr Helby was killed earlier in the year.

In 1924, three years after the two accidents took place, a woman who is a psychic saw one of the 'hairy hands' about a mile west of the place where the accidents occurred. She and her husband were in a caravan near the ruins of Powder Mills, about half a mile to the north of the road. She awoke with a start one cold moonlit night, with a strong feeling that there was something highly dangerous close at hand …

"I knew there was some power very seriously menacing us, and I must act swiftly. As I looked up to the little window at the end of the caravan, I saw something moving, and as I stared, my heart beating fast, I saw it was the fingers and palm of a very large hand, with many hairs on the joints and the back of it, clawing up and up to the top of the window, which was a little open.

I knew it wished to do harm to my husband sleeping below. I knew that the owner of the hand hated us, and wished us harm, and I knew it was no ordinary human hand, and that no blow or shot would have any power over it. Almost unconsciously, I made the sign of the Cross and I prayed very much that we might be kept safe from harm. At once the hand slowly sank down out of sight, and I knew the danger had gone. I never felt the evil influence again near the caravan …"

To the sceptical mind, many questions are left unanswered by this story. What evidence was there that the doctor's accident had anything to do with ghostly hands? None is offered. And the young army officer; couldn't he have been using the hairy hands story to cover a stupid and embarrassing accident brought on himself by careless driving on a nasty bank? Of course, his explanation could be honest to the last word. But, *as reported*, doesn't his speech sound just too well-composed to be true? Does anyone in a state of shock after a road crash speak in such dramatically sculptured sentences? As for the psychic lady, she wakes in the night and sees a sight that *she might expect to see if the hairy hands legend were true* … Though I have to admit that the hairy hands could exist (there is no evidence of a scientific kind that they do, but equally, there is none that they don't), I am making the point that the 'psychic' lady was the kind of person whose worries and fears come before her as ghost-like figures which she truly believes she 'sees'. And those imagined figures take the shape of whatever ghost she hears about and which is supposed to haunt the place where she is at any one time. This is quite as likely as the possibility that she was indeed psychic and possessed the power of perceiving what others do not. The trouble is that the story does not supply any evidence which helps us decide the truth about her. And so we have to say that, interesting though the story is, it is not very much use as evidence for or against the existence of ghosts, nor does it help us to understand them if they do exist.

 Comprehension **A**
1 How was Dr Helby travelling across Dartmoor?
2 Why did the young officer leave the house of his friend?
3 Why did he return an hour later?
4 How did the psychic woman feel when she woke up?
5 What did she 'see'?

B
1 Why do you think 'a queer look came into the young officer's eyes' when his friend asked him what had happened?
2 Why do you think the writer says that the psychic woman's story does not provide any evidence either for or against the existence of ghosts?
3 Explain each of these words or phrases in your own words.
   a at a considerable distance
   b psychic
   c seriously menacing
   d the sceptical mind

C Carefully read the passage again. The passage gives information about three incidents:

- Doctor Helby's accident
- the young officer's accident
- the psychic woman's experience.

For each incident, say whether the writer is convinced or not convinced that the hairy hands were to blame for what happened and suggest a reason for his opinion.

Vocabulary

Presenting an argument

When you are **presenting an argument** that you hope will persuade your reader to see your point of view, there are several words and phrases that are useful. For example:

I believe that …
It is my opinion that …

A Each of the incomplete sentences below begins with a phrase that is useful for expressing an opinion. Copy and complete each sentence, expressing your opinion about ghosts.

1 In my opinion _____ .

2 My reasons for thinking _____ .

3 The evidence leads me to this point of view because

_____ .

4 On the other hand, _____ .

5 In conclusion, _____ .

B Use each word from the box in a persuasive sentence of your own. You may need to look up some up of the words in a dictionary.

consider	therefore	evidence	nevertheless	reason	belief

Spelling

Syllables

Remember, words can be divided into **syllables**, which can help with your spelling. A syllable is a part of a word that has its own vowel sound. When we say words, we emphasise, or stress, some syllables more than others. For example, say these two two-syllable words to yourself:

transmit

limit

When we say 'transmit', we stress the second syllable, 'mit'.

When we say 'limit', we stress the first syllable, 'lim'.

A Copy each word below and draw circles or lines to divide it into its syllables (if it has more than one syllable). Underline the words whose last, or only, syllable is stressed.

1 dig	2 wallow	3 public	4 comic
5 jump	6 reveal	7 selfish	8 commit

When adding a **suffix** to a one-syllable word, or one whose last syllable is stressed, look at the letter before the last one. If it is a vowel and does not have another vowel beside it, we usually double the last letter before adding the suffix. For example:

hop	(letter before last is a vowel)	hopping
omit	(last syllable is stressed)	omitting
transmit	(last syllable is stressed)	transmitted
propel	(last syllable is stressed)	propelling

If:

* the letter before the last one is not a vowel
* the letter before the last one has a vowel beside it
* the last syllable of the word is unstressed

we usually just add the suffix. For example:

sing	singing
read	reading
profit (last syllable is not stressed)	profited

This tip doesn't work for words ending with 'w', 'x' or 'y', which are never doubled. For example:

box	boxed	boxing
mow	mowed	mowing

B Copy and complete this table. First, underline the stressed syllable and circle the letter before last in each word.

	Add 'ing'	Add 'ed'
return	returning	returned
resist		
admit		
benefit		
suggest		

Grammar

Active and passive sentences

Remember, some **passive sentences** don't say who or what is doing the action of the verb to the subject. For example:

The <u>motor bike</u> was <u>ridden</u> along the road.

| subject | | passive verb |

We know that the action of the verb was done to the subject, but we don't know by whom/what. The sentence could have read:

The motorbike <u>was ridden</u> along the road by Doctor Helby.

A Copy these passive sentences, changing them so that each sentence does not say who or what did the action.

1 The young officer was driven off the road by a pair of hairy hands.

2 The doctor was hurled off the motorbike by a strange force.

3 He was killed instantly by the force with which he hit the road.

B Now rewrite each of the sentences from part A as an active sentence. The first one has been done to help you.

1 A pair of hairy hands drove the young officer off the road.

Sentence construction

Conditional sentences

A sentence is a **conditional sentence** if one action depends upon another. For example:

I might believe in ghosts if I had seen one.

I will find out more about such mysteries if I can find a suitable book at the library.

A Complete these conditional sentences.

1 Doctor Helby wouldn't have been killed if _____ .

2 The young officer's accident wouldn't have been significant if _____ .

3 The psychic woman was sure her husband would have been harmed if _____ .

4 There is no way of knowing if _____ .

B Complete each conditional sentence by adding a main clause.

1 _____ if they were out after dark on the moor.

2 _____ if there was an unexplained accident.

3 _____ if they could avoid it.

4 _____ if I was in their position.

Writing

Examining the evidence

The passage on pages 52–54 is one of many accounts in *Aidan Chambers' Book of Ghosts and Hauntings*, in which the author **examines the evidence** for the existence of ghosts. His conclusion after reading the reports about the hairy hands is that they provide no evidence about whether ghosts do or do not exist. He puts forward reasonable explanations for the things that occurred. For him, the evidence is inconclusive.

Other people reading the reports might be convinced that the hairy hands did exist, perhaps because so many strange things happened in that part of Devon. They would feel that the evidence in the reports supported the argument that ghosts exist.

You are going to write a report about a supposed sighting of a ghost in a deserted house. Use your imagination to:

- give details of where the house is and what it looks like
- recount at least three sightings of the ghost by different people – quote the people's own words as Aidan Chambers did in 'The Hairy Hands'.

Write your opinion as to whether the evidence of these sightings provides conclusive proof that the ghost exists, or whether they are inconclusive. Give an ordinary explanation for at least one of the sightings.

Write a draft of your work. Check the draft to ensure that you have given precise details of each of the sightings and the conclusion you draw from the evidence. Proofread and revise your first draft, then write out your final copy.

The Highway Code

The Highway Code is a booklet which sets out the rules for all road-users – pedestrians, horse riders and cyclists, as well as motorcyclists and drivers. This section is about animals.

Rules about animals

Horseriders

34. Safety equipment. Children under the age of 14 MUST wear a helmet which complies with the Regulations. It MUST be fastened securely. Other riders should also follow this advice.

35. Other clothing. You should wear
- boots or shoes with hard soles and heels
- light-coloured or fluorescent clothing in daylight
- reflective clothing if you have to ride at night or in poor visibility.

36. At night. It is safer not to ride on the road at night or in poor visibility, but if you do, make sure your horse has reflective bands above the fetlock joints. Carry a light which shows white to the front and red to the rear.

Riding

37. Before you take a horse on to a road, you should
- ensure all tack fits well and is in good condition
- make sure you can control the horse.

Always ride with other, less nervous horses if you think that your horse will be nervous of traffic. Never ride a horse without a saddle or bridle.

38. Before riding off or turning, look behind you to make sure it is safe, then give a clear arm signal.

39. When riding on the road you should
- keep to the left
- keep both hands on the reins unless you are signalling
- keep both feet in the stirrups
- not carry another person
- not carry anything which might affect your balance or get tangled up with the reins
- keep a horse you are leading to your left

- move in the direction of the traffic flow in a one-way street
- never ride more than two abreast, and ride in single file where the road narrows or on the approach to a bend.

40. You MUST NOT take a horse on to a footpath, pavement or cycle track. Use a bridleway where possible.

41. Avoid roundabouts wherever possible. If you use them you should

- keep to the left and watch out for vehicles crossing your path to leave or join the roundabout
- signal right when riding across exits to show you are not leaving
- signal left just before you leave the roundabout.

Other animals

42. Dogs. Do not let a dog out on the road on its own. Keep it on a short lead when walking on the pavement, road or path shared with cyclists.

43. When in a vehicle make sure dogs or other animals are suitably restrained so they cannot distract you while you are driving or injure you if you stop quickly.

44. Animals being herded. These should be kept under control at all times. You should, if possible, send another person along the road in front to warn other road users, especially at a bend or the brow of a hill. It is safer not to move animals after dark, but if you do, then wear reflective clothing and ensure that lights are carried (white at the front and red at the rear of the herd).

Comprehension

A

1 What must children under 14 wear when riding?
2 What should horseriders wear at night or in poor visibility?
3 What two things should horseriders do before riding off or turning?
4 If you are leading a horse, on which side of you should it be?
5 When herding animals, when and how should lights be used?

B

1 Why do you think some of the instructions say 'MUST' and some say 'should'?
2 Why do you think *The Highway Code* says horseriders should 'Avoid roundabouts wherever possible'?
3 Why do you think a dog should not be let out on the road on its own?
4 Why do you think a dog should be kept on a short lead?
5 Why does it say that horseriders should 'use a bridleway where possible'?

C Find the following words and phrases in 'Rules about animals'. For each one, write down a word or phrase that could have been used instead.

1 complies with
2 fastened securely
3 reflective clothing
4 poor visibility
5 abreast
6 suitably restrained

Vocabulary

Presenting an argument

Remember, when you are **presenting an argument** that you hope will persuade your reader to see your point of view, there are several useful words and phrases that are useful. For example:

I firmly believe …   In my opinion …   That is no reason …

A Write a short passage, putting forward your opinion about whether or not cyclists should take a test before being allowed to ride a bicycle on the road. Use some of the words and phrases from the box below to help you.

> believe   opinion   whereas   besides   although
> nonetheless   thus   despite   conclusion
> on the other hand   in spite of

Use your dictionary to look up any words you are unsure about.

B Use all the words from the box below in a paragraph of your own giving your opinion about whether people should be allowed to ride horses on roads.

> consequently   contention   furthermore   inevitable

Spelling

'ary' and 'ery'

Most words ending with 'ry' that are adjectives or nouns referring to people end with '**ary**'. For example:

adjective: imagin<u>ary</u>
'person' noun: mission<u>ary</u>

Most words ending with 'ry' that are nouns end with '**ery**'. For example:
    machin<u>ery</u>

Some adjectives end in 'ery' if their root word ends with 'e' or 'er'. For example:

slave   slav<u>ery</u>
thunder   thund<u>ery</u>

But, as with all spelling rules, there are exceptions! For example:

adjective: slipp<u>ery</u>
noun: libr<u>ary</u>

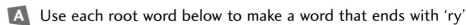

A Use each root word below to make a word that ends with 'ry'

1	flatter	2	powder	3	water
4	baker	5	grocer	6	bribe
7	discover	8	deliver	9	recover

B Complete each word by adding 'ary' or 'ery'.

1	secret___	2	nurs___	3	necess___
4	ordin___	5	batt___	6	myst___
7	compliment___	8	prim___	9	revolution___

Grammar

Imperative sentences

Official documents usually tell us what to do. They use **imperative sentences**. For example:

> <u>Keep</u> to the left
>
> <u>Avoid</u> roundabouts

The main verb usually comes at the beginning of an imperative sentence.

Sometimes, an imperative can be made negative by adding 'Never' or 'Don't' at the beginning of the instruction. For example:

> <u>Never</u> ride more than two abreast.

A Rewrite each sentence twice using the imperative, the first time positively, and the next time negatively. The first one has been done to help you.

1 It is always sensible to wear a helmet when riding a horse or bike.

Wear a helmet whenever you ride a horse or a bike.

Never ride a horse or bike without wearing a helmet.

Safety First unit 8

64

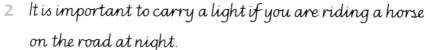

2   It is important to carry a light if you are riding a horse on the road at night.

3   When you are about to cross the road, look and listen carefully for traffic.

4   If you are riding a horse on the road, you should ensure that you are in control of your animal.

Imperative sentences can be turned into requests by inserting 'please', which can usually be added at various points in the sentence. For example:

<u>Please</u> get out your homework.

Get out your homework <u>please</u>.

<u>Please</u> open your books and copy the questions.

Open your books, <u>please</u>, and copy the questions.

Put away the equipment, <u>please</u>.

Adding 'please' is not necessarily a politeness; 'please' can make an instruction even more demanding.

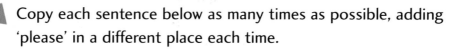 **B** Copy each sentence below as many times as possible, adding 'please' in a different place each time.

1   Don't walk on the grass.

2   Stop talking immediately.

3   Cross busy roads carefully.

4   Look and listen before you cross.

Sentence construction

Editing

It is important to read your writing and **edit** it, correcting and improving it before showing it to other people. You need to check:

- spelling
- punctuation
- whether you could have used better, more interesting words
- whether there is any repetition or any unnecessary words
- that there are no double negatives
- whether the words and phrases are in the best order
- whether you need to add more detail.

A Copy and improve each sentence, using more descriptive words and phrases.

1 I got a nice surprise when I woke up at Christmas.

2 A bike was at the bottom of my bed.

3 There was nothing I could do but laugh and cry when I saw it.

4 It was a good bike.

5 I went out on my bike.

B Edit the following sentences, checking all the things mentioned above, and copy the edited version of each one.

1 As most people know, rideing bikes at night can be very very dangerous and especialy if the person riding the bike is a person whoisn't used to it and doesn't not have any good lights

2 wen you are thinking that you might be about to cross a road look for the safest place not never near a blind, bend lisen very carfully for any veicles coming and look to see if you can see any veicles coming along the road.

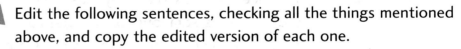

Writing

Official language

Information writing that gives instructions or important information is usually written in very precise, **official language** so there can be no misunderstanding.

The Highway Code is a document of this type, and the language it contains is very specific. For example:

- It does not say 'wear something on your head', because it does not want people to think that a woolly hat or cap is suitable. It says: '... wear a helmet which complies with the Regulations'. There can be no misunderstandings.
- It does not say 'Wear proper footwear.' It says 'You should wear boots or shoes with hard soles and heels.'

Imagine you have been asked to write two leaflets for your local sports centre.

1 The first leaflet is a list of precise rules as to how members must dress and behave while in the sports centre.
2 The second leaflet contains precise information about the times of opening, prices and what the sports centre has to offer.

Remember to be precise and choose your words carefully. For example telling someone they must wear sports shoes is not very helpful; they may need to know that they must wear shoes that will not mark the courts. Telling someone that no glass bottles are allowed is not precise enough if you only mean that no glass bottles are allowed around the swimming-pool area.

Draft your leaflets first and then proofread and revise them, before writing your final copy.

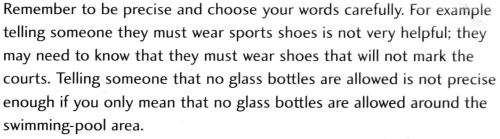

Sport in Ancient Greece

Read the information about Ancient Greece in the four book extracts below.

Life in Ancient Greece

Mary Gardiner

In Ancient Greece there were many sports competitions but the four biggest ones were known as the Panhellenic Games.

Men came from all over the Greek world to take part (women were not allowed to compete in the men's games). Many buildings were erected for the Games. These were for housing the competitors and important people who came to watch, and for performing religious ceremonies. At Olympia, a huge statue was erected of Zeus, the king of the gods. It was about 13 metres high and was one of the Seven Wonders of the Ancient World.

The Ancient Greeks

John Turner

The Olympic Games were held in honour of the god Zeus. No one knows exactly when the Olympic Games began, but official records date back to 776 BC. At first, there was only one event – running – but, later, others were added, including wrestling, boxing, chariot racing, horse racing and the pentathlon – an event with five separate parts. There was an enormous feast on the last day, and the winners were presented with palm branches, olive wreaths or woollen ribbons. If any athlete had performed really well, a statue was put up in his honour.

Of all the Panhellenic competitions of Ancient Greece, the Olympic Games were the most important. Held in Olympia, a city sacred to the god Zeus, the Olympiad, as the games were called, was part of an important religious festival.

The Games took place every four years for a period of over 1,000 years, but ended when Olympia was destroyed by earthquakes in AD 395. At first, the games lasted just one day but, from the seventy-seventh Olympiad, they were extended to five days.

The History of the Olympic Games

B. J. Brownlow

Great Warriors

I. Brawl

There were many local sports competitions held in Ancient Greece. It was very important for the men to be fit, as they had to be prepared for battle in the many wars between states within the Greek empire. Every four years, when the Olympic Games were due to begin, messengers travelled throughout the empire, commanding that all wars between states should stop so that the competitors and spectators could safely gather at Olympia for the games.

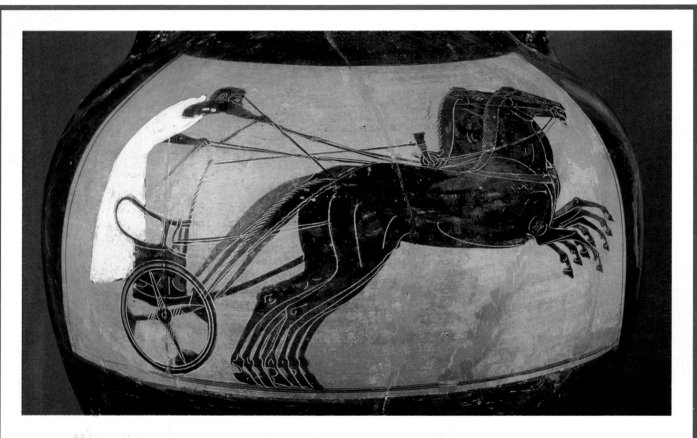

 Comprehension **A**

1 How many major competitions made up the Panhellenic Games?

2 When did official records of the Olympic Games begin?

3 What were the uses of the buildings erected for the Games?

4 Which two events involved horses?

5 Where were the Olympic Games held?

6 Why were athletic competitions important in Ancient Greece?

B

1 The prizes awarded to the winners do not seem very special to us today. Why do you think the athletes were eager to take part in the Games?

2 Why do you think temples and statues to the gods were associated with the Games?

3 How do you think we know so much about the early Olympic Games, which took place well over 2,000 years ago?

C Quickly skim the information from the four books and make notes on anything to do with the types of events in the Games.

Vocabulary

Prefixes

You have learned that many English words come from other languages. For example:

athlon is the Greek word for 'contest'

Many **prefixes** come from Greek or Latin words for numbers. For example:

deci comes from the Latin word *decem*, which means 'tenth' or 'ten'

So, 'decathlon' means 'a contest in ten parts'.

A Each word below starts with a prefix that stands for a number. Copy the definition of each word, filling in the missing number. Use your dictionary to help you.

Word	Definition
triathlon	a sports event with _____ parts
pentathlon	a sports event with _____ parts
octagon	a shape with _____ sides and angles
hexagon	a shape with _____ sides and angles
bicycle	a vehicle with _____ wheels
tricycle	a vehicle with _____ wheels
century	_____ years
biennial	occurring every _____ years
decade	_____ years
millennium	_____ years
quadruped	an animal with _____ legs
triplets	_____ babies, born at the same time
sextuplets	_____ babies, born at the same time

B Using the information from part A, make up eight words of your own (with definitions) using number prefixes. They can be as silly as you like! For example:

a bitrunkephant – an elephant with two trunks

Spelling

'f' and 'fe' endings

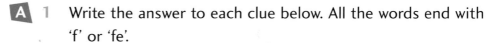

Remember, to make the plurals of nouns that end in '**f**' or '**fe**', we usually change the 'f' or 'fe' to a 'v', and add 'es'. For example:

    wolf   wol<u>ves</u>

    li<u>fe</u>   li<u>ves</u>

There are several exceptions to the rule. For example:

    religious belie<u>f</u>   religious belief<u>s</u>

    coral ree<u>f</u>   coral reef<u>s</u>

A 1 Write the answer to each clue below. All the words end with 'f' or 'fe'.

    a a person who steals

    b the young of a cow

    c the partner of a husband

    d a bundle of wheat

    e for blowing your nose on

    f a horse's foot

    g for keeping your neck warm

    h used to cut with

    i leader of a tribe

    j attached to a wall for holding books and ornaments

2 Write the plural of each answer from question 1. Check the spellings in a dictionary.

B Write down the plurals from question 2 of part A that were exceptions to the rule. Try to work out a rule for these words.

Grammar

Verb tenses

Different types of writing require different **verb tenses** but, remember, there are more ways of making the different tenses than adding 's', 'ing' or 'ed'. 'Helper', or auxiliary, verbs can be used. For example:

Verb family	Past tense	Present tense	Future tense
to smile	she smiled she was smiling	she smiles she is smiling	she will smile

In the example, 'she was smiling' is called the **past continuous tense** and 'she is smiling' is called the **present continuous tense**.

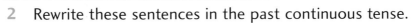

Be careful! Some of these verbs are **irregular** – they change rather than having the suffix 'ed' or 'ing' added.

A 1 Copy and complete this table.

Verb family	Past tense	Present tense	Future tense
to laugh	she laughed she was laughing	she laughs she is laughing	she will laugh
to compete	they _____ they ____ ____	they _____ they ____ ____	they ____ ____
to swim	we _____ we ____ ____	we _____ we ____ ____	we ____ ____
to think	you _____ you ____ ____	you _____ you ____ ____	you ____ ____

2 Rewrite these sentences in the past continuous tense.

a Dan watches as Patrick, competes in the race.

b Patrick runs the race of his life.

c Dan yells with excitement.

d Patrick crosses the line first, as the crowd cheers.

e Dan runs to congratulate him.

f They wave as the crowd applauds.

B Write a sentence to explain why you think the past continuous tense and the present continuous tense were given those names.

Sentence construction

Phrase and clause order

Remember, **adverbs** tell us how, when or where the action of a verb takes place.

You have learned about complex sentences and different types of clauses. You can improve your writing by thinking about the **order** of the phrases and clauses in complex sentences. For example:

Probably one of the greatest ever sprinters was clearly disturbed by the crowd who were quite unaware that a race was about to begin and were cheering the pole-vaulters.

The sentence can be improved by rearranging the clauses. For example:

The sprinter, probably one of the greatest ever, was clearly disturbed by the crowd who, quite unaware that a race was about to begin, were cheering the pole-vaulters.

A Rearrange each of these sentences in at least two other ways, putting a tick against the version you prefer. You may need to make some other minor changes.

1 As the relay team received their medals it was clear from their faces that, coming as they did from a country lacking adequate training facilities, the victory meant a great deal.

2 Taking his last throw, the athlete, holding the javelin above his head, gave a great shout and, with an expression of intense concentration, thundered towards the line.

B Write a complex sentence about the Olympics. Rearrange it in as many ways as you can, putting a tick against the version you think is best.

Writing

Paragraphs

If you were going to write a factual account of the Olympic Games in Ancient Greece, you would need to plan your work as follows.

Stage 1: Research
You would need to find reference books, encyclopaedias and, perhaps, CD-ROMs, which would contain information about the topic.

Stage 2: Making notes
You would need to make notes from these sources, keeping a record of the sources you use, so that you can acknowledge them.

Ancient Greece unit 9

Here are the sort of notes you could make from the four extracts on pages 68–69:

Life in Ancient Greece

4 major competitions – Panhellenic Games
   people came from all over Greek world
women not allowed to take part
buildings – for competitors, important
   people, religious ceremonies
statue of Zeus, Olympia – about 13 m high;
   one of Seven Wonders of Ancient World

The Ancient Greeks

official records kept from 776 BC
events – at first, only running, then
   wrestling, boxing, chariot racing, horse
   racing, pentathlon
feast at the end
prizes – olive wreaths, palm branches,
   woollen ribbons; statues in honour of
   top athletes

The History of the Olympic Games

Olympics – most important of Panhellenic
   Games
held in Olympia, city sacred to Zeus
Olympiad part of religious festival
Games every four years for 1,000 + years
until 77th Olympiad, games lasted 1 day,
   then 5 days
Olympia destroyed by earthquake in AD 395

Great Warriors

lots of local sports competitions
important for men to be fit – had to go
   to war
before the Games began, messengers
   ordered wars to stop

Stage 3: Sorting your notes

In the notes above, the information is sorted by book title. The next stage would be to group the information together under headings.

Stage 4: Planning your report

Having sorted the information into sections, you would need to decide the order in which to present the information, and organise the material into paragraphs. For example:

paragraph 1: why athletics was important   **paragraph 2**: the Panhellenic Games
paragraph 3: the Olympic Games   **paragraph 4**: buildings
paragraph 5: competitions and prizes

1   Sort the notes from the box above into five sections.
2   Using the notes you have sorted and the suggested paragraph plan in stage 4, write a factual account of sport in Ancient Greece. When you have finished the first draft, carefully check the spelling, punctuation, and content. Revise your report, and prepare your final copy, including a title.

Cliffs Under Attack

Where the land and the sea meet, we often find cliffs. Cliffs, like all the land under our feet, may be made from hard, tough rocks, such as granite, or from softer rocks, such as limestone. Some cliffs are made from a mixture of rock types.

As the bottom of a cliff is pounded by the waves, it is gradually worn away. Water is forced into cracks in the cliffs at wave height, the cracks widen and, eventually, pieces break away. These fall into the water, where they are churned about in the waves, constantly rubbing against one another, and gradually breaking down into smaller rocks, then pebbles (or shingle) and, eventually, fine sand.

If you examine the sand on a beach, you may find it is similar in colour to the rocks in nearby cliffs. If the beach comes from yellow

or red sandstone, it will have yellow sand. If the cliffs are made from limestone, the sand is white and, if the cliffs are made from volcanic lava rock, the beach may be black!

Sometimes, there is no beach on a rocky headland. As soon as pieces of rock and sand are washed from the cliff, they are carried away by the powerful waves and currents, to be washed up further down the coast.

Waves gradually wear away cliffs, even those of the hardest rock, as the water enters where thay are slightly weaker. Where this happens, a cave may be formed. The cave gradually becomes larger until it forms an arch. Eventually, the roof of an arch will collapse, leaving a pillar of rock known as a stack.

In the photo on the top right, you can see a cave on the left of the picture. Next to it is an arch and, on the right, a stack. In the picture below, you can see a number of stacks that have formed along a stretch of coast, as well as shingle and rocks, formed as the cliffs are broken down by the waves.

Comprehension **A** Write a sentence to answer each question.

1 Give an example of a hard rock.
2 Give an example of a soft rock.
3 What is another word for 'pebbles'?
4 What colour is a beach made from volcanic lava rocks?
5 How do waves affect rocks?

B 1 Find two examples of passive sentences in the passage.
2 Why do you think the passage is written in the present tense?
3 What do you think is the purpose of this piece of writing?
4 Who do you think it is written for?

C In your own words, write an explanation of each of the following.
1 how the rocks at the base of a cliff are weakened
2 how sand is formed
3 how a stack is formed

Vocabulary

Roots, prefixes and suffixes

Remember, words are often made from **roots**, **prefixes** and **suffixes**. Knowing the meanings of common roots, prefixes and suffixes can help you work out what words mean. For example:

Prefix		**Root**	
sub	+	marine	= submarine
meaning 'under' or 'below		meaning 'of the sea', from the Latin word for sea, *mare*	an adjective meaning 'existing under the sea', or a noun meaning 'a vessel that travels under the sea'

A Mix and match prefixes, suffixes and roots to invent six new words of your own. For example:

> 'anti' + school = antischool (not liking school)
>
> 'homework' + less = homeworkless (having no homework)

Choose prefixes and suffixes from the boxes below to help you. Use your dictionary to check their meanings if you are not sure.

Prefixes
un anti dis inter im sub in
super ultra mis pre tele ex fore

Suffixes
ion ment ly ness ure ful less
ty ance ence

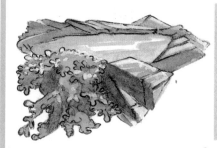

A **compound word** is a word made by joining two other words. For example:

> sea + weed = seaweed   sand + castle = sandcastle
>
> skate + board = skateboard   drain + pipe = drainpipe
>
> farm + yard = farmyard   post + box = postbox

B Make up five new compound words of your own. For example:

> head + sock = headsock (another name for a hat!)
>
> hand + ache = handache (what you might get if you've been doing a lot of writing!)

You could choose words from the box and think of other words to add to them, or you can make up your own word combinations.

foot head book rain dog coat house school
party friend bag box car bike holiday

Spelling

Prefixes

There are many rules about adding suffixes to words. Sometimes, you have to alter or drop one or more letters. However, when adding a **prefix**, the only rule is: just add it! Don't miss out any letters. For example:

'un' + sure = unsure

Sometimes, adding a prefix creates a double letter. For example:

'dis' + satisfy = di<u>ss</u>atisfy

The prefix ends with 's' and the word to which it is being added begins with an 's', which creates a double 's'. Don't be tempted to leave one out.

A List all the words that have double letters as a result of adding these prefixes.

1	dis +	service	organise	appear
		trust	similar	obey
2	un +	necessary	invited	eventful
		numbered	natural	named
3	over +	reach	turn	rule
		ride	look	run
4	im +	movable	possible	mortal
		modest	moral	measurable

B Write a word that uses each of the following prefixes, and whose root begins with the same letter as the last letter of the prefix. Use each word in a sentence of your own. Use your dictionary to help you.

1 mis   2 inter   3 pre   4 re

Grammar

Idiom origins

Remember, **idioms** are expressions we use to help us describe things or situations. There are dictionaries that provide information about why and when these sayings were first used. For example, here is an extract from *The Cassell Dictionary of Word and Phrase Origins*:

> **hat in the ring.** *See* THROW ONE'S ...
>
> **hatter.** *See* MAD AS A ...
>
> **have a cat in Hell's chance, not to.** Meaning 'to have no chance whatsoever', the full expression makes the phrase clear: 'No more chance than a cat in hell *without claws'*, which is recorded in Grose, *Dictionary of the Vulgar Tongue* (1796).
>
> **have a chip on one's shoulder, to.** Meaning 'to bear a grudge in a defensive manner', the expression originated in the USA where it was known by the early nineteenth century. A boy or man would, or would seem, to carry a chip (of wood) on his shoulder daring others to dislodge it, looking for a fight.
>
> **have a feather in one's cap, to.** Meaning '[to have] an honour or achievement of which one can be proud'. The expression (known by 1700) probably dates from 1346, when the Black Prince was awarded the crest of John, King of Bohemia, which showed three ostrich feathers, after he had distinguished himself at the Battle of Crécy. This symbol has since been carried by every Prince of Wales. Later, any knight who had fought well might wear a feather in his helmet.

A What do you think each of these sentences really means?

1 I knew we wouldn't stand a cat in Hell's chance if we were caught in the cave when the tide came in.

2 Passing the geography test was a real feather in his cap.

3 She had a chip on her shoulder because she had not been accepted into the Science Club.

B Research the possible origin and meaning of each expression. If you don't have a suitable reference book, try looking up the key words in your dictionary. If you cannot find the information, see if you can work out the meaning from the rest of the sentence.

1 "Now the balloon will go up!" exclaimed John, as Vince stormed into the room.

2 "You're barking up the wrong tree," said John when Vince confronted him.

3 "You'll eat your heart out when you know where I've been," said Sally smugly.

Punctuation

Letters

Here are two **letters** written by the same person but to different people, and for different reasons. When you write a letter, the vocabulary and 'tone' of the letter should be based on the purpose of the letter, and what effect you want it to have on the reader.

A Rewrite the following personal letter correctly. You will need to think about:

- the correct way to set out a letter
- paragraphs
- capital letters
- punctuation.

23 centre crescent

blaxland

essex

15th July

dear grandma

here we are on holiday mum and i arrived on the coach yesterday we cant wait to go in the sea but it has been too cold so far we went for a long walk along the beach towards fishermans cove paddling as we went it was great fun at first but it was really frightening when suddenly a large portion of cliff gave way with no warning it was a wonder that no one on the beach was badly hurt we were all very lucky i dont think well go near those cliffs again well thats enough for now i am just going to get fish and chips with mum please give my love to aunty diane and uncle richard and tell my cousins that im really excited about seeing them again soon with love freya

This is the formal letter that Freya wrote to the Council after her holiday. Again, rewrite the letter correctly, considering the points in part A.

23 centre crescent

blaxland

essex

10th September

the chief executive

beachville council

overdown road

beachville

northshire

dear sir/madam

i should like to make a complaint about the dangerous state of the cliffs near fishermans cove when i was walking along the beach with my mother a few weeks ago we were very nearly hit by large rocks falling from the cliffs whilst i accept that the council cannot prevent the collapse of the cliffs i do think it is important and certainly the councils responsibility to ensure that there are warning signs in the area i look forward to hearing what you intend to do about this situation which my mother and i consider a matter of great urgency yours faithfully freya smith

Writing

Explanations

'Cliffs Under Attack' is a piece of non-fiction writing which explains how something happens. **Explanations** like this are often written in the present tense and use passive sentences.

This is the structure of the passage:

Paragraph 1 introduces the text and lets the reader know what the passage is about

Paragraph 2 explains how cliffs are worn away

Paragraph 3 explains why sand is different colours

Paragraph 4 explains how caves are formed

Paragraph 5 explains how sea stacks are formed.

The photographs help the reader to understand what is being explained.

A The author could have used diagrams instead of photographs to go with the text. Look carefully at the photographs on pages 76–77. Draw annotated (labelled) diagrams to explain what is happening in each picture.

B Choose one of the following:

- Waterfalls – How are waterfalls formed?
- Rivers – What are river terraces and how are they made?
- Rainfall – Why does it rain more in the west of Britain than in the east?

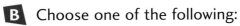

1 Research your chosen topic and make notes.
2 Plan the structure of your explanation. You will need an introductory paragraph so the reader knows what is being explained. Order your notes into paragraphs that take the reader through your explanation step-by-step.
3 Include diagrams to help the reader.
4 Write your first draft, then proofread and revise it.
5 Write your final copy, add a suitable title and a bibliography.

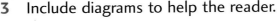

Tutankhamun's Gold

Howard Carter was growing desperate. For nearly 20 years he had searched for the tomb of the Ancient Egyptian boy king, Tutankhamun. Now, money to finance his quest was running out ...

What made the prospect of failure harder to bear was that the English scholar remained convinced that the tomb was somewhere in the Valley of the Kings, site of the ancient capital of Thebes, for there were many inscriptions about Tutankhamun in the nearby temple of Luxor. He believed, too, that the tomb had never been looted, for no relics had ever been reported.

Ancient Egypt

From about 3100 BC, for 3,000 years, Egypt was a powerful country. Over that period, it had 300 rulers, known as pharaohs, whose people worshipped them as living gods. Tutankhamun is thought to have ruled in Egypt in the thirteenth century BC. He was only a boy when he came to the throne and he died ten years later. Although we know little about him, he is probably one of the most famous pharaohs, thanks to Carter's discovery of his magnificent tomb.

But all he had found – 15 years before – were jars of clothes bearing the king's name. Since then, Carter had explored nearly the whole floor of the valley and found no trace of the pharaoh who had died at the age of 18 in 1323 BC.

As Carter trudged through the dawn-cool sand to his diggings, he thought again of his patron, the amateur archaeologist, Lord Carnarvon, and remembered their last meeting in England. Carnarvon had wanted to call off the search. "It has cost me a fortune," he told Carter. "I can't afford it."

But Carter pleaded with him to finance one last try. "All right, Howard," Carnarvon laughed. "I'm a gambler. I'll back you for one more toss. If it is a loss, then I am

through. Where do we begin?" Carter showed him a map of the valley, indicating a small triangular area not yet explored as it was on the approach to the tomb of Ramses VI. "There," he told his patron. "It's the last place left."

Now, as he approached his diggings, Carter reflected that this looked like a dismal end to his dream. He and his workmen had found nothing but the rubble of huts which had been used by labourers building the tomb of Ramses. For three days they had hacked at the rubble and found nothing.

When Carter reached the site, his foreman, Ali, ran over. "We have uncovered a step cut into the ground," he said. Within two days they had cleared a steep staircase that led down to a sealed door. Carter immediately sent a telegram to Carnarvon:

```
AT LAST HAVE MADE WONDERFUL DISCOVERY IN
VALLEY STOP A MAGNIFICENT TOMB WITH SEALS
INTACT STOP RE-COVERED SAME FOR YOUR ARRIVAL
CONGRATULATIONS
```

The date was 6th November, 1922.

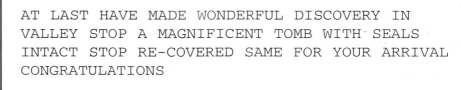

Carter wrote later about his first sight of the inside of the tomb:
At first I could see nothing, the hot air from the chamber causing the candle flames to flicker. But as my eyes grew accustomed to the light, details of the room emerged slowly from the mist; strange animals, statues and gold – everywhere the glint of gold. For the moment – an eternity it must have seemed to others standing by – I was struck dumb with amazement; and when Lord Carnarvon, unable to stand the suspense any longer, inquired anxiously, "Can you see anything?" it was all I could do to get out the words, "Yes – wonderful things."

Comprehension **A**

1 Who was paying for Howard Carter to search for the tomb of Tutankhamun?

2 Where did Howard Carter believe Tutankhamun's tomb to be and why?

3 Why was he so sure the tomb had never been looted?

4 Where was the part of the Valley of the Kings which Carter had not yet explored?

5 How did Howard Carter first learn that a breakthrough had been made?

B

1 Why do you think it was so important to Carter that the seals of the tomb were intact?

2 Why do you think Carter did not immediately open the tomb?

3 When Carter first entered the tomb, why do you think it would have seemed 'an eternity' for those behind him?

4 Why do you think Carnarvon inquired 'anxiously' whether Carter could see anything?

5 Write in your own words what Carter felt when he first looked into the tomb.

C

1 Make a list of the different ways in which the writer has presented the information.

2 Where do you think you would find a piece of writing like this?

 Vocabulary

Over-used words

Remember, it is important to check and revise your writing to see if you can improve it. One way of improving your writing is to avoid **over-used words** and replace them with more interesting and descriptive words. For example:

Howard Carter <u>said</u> that he had made a <u>good</u> discovery.

'Said' and 'good' are two over-used words, and there are usually better words to use instead. For example:

Howard Carter <u>announced</u> that he had made an <u>intriguing</u> discovery.

A Rewrite these sentences and improve them by replacing the coloured words with more interesting words. You may need to change one or two other words as well.

1 Carter asked for more time to look for the tomb.

2 Lord Carnarvon was a nice man, and he said that Carter could have one more go.

3 He had already spent a lot of money, hoping to make a big discovery.

4 "Carter has got a lot of determination," Lord Carnarvon said to a friend.

5 "I'm sure he'll soon get you a big reward," said the friend.

B Look again at your answers to part A. Think about any other improvements you could make to the sentences, and write them down.

Spelling

Plurals – words ending with 'o'

Remember, to make the **plural** of nouns that end with 'o', we usually add 'es'. For example:

tomato   tomato**es**

However, words that are abbreviations (shortened forms of words), music words and words ending in 'oo' are all made plural by adding 's'. For example:

abbreviation: rhino**s** ('rhino' is short for 'rhinoceros')
music word: cello**s**
word ending with 'oo':   cuckoo**s**

A Write the plural form of each of these nouns. Remember the guidelines, and use a dictionary if you are unsure of the meaning of any of the words.

1 soprano	2 hero	3 volcano
4 dingo	5 contralto	6 motto
7 radio	8 cockatoo	9 cello
10 echo	11 piccolo	12 skidoo

B Copy and complete this word puzzle. All the answers should be plural.

1 vegetables that grow under the ground

2 pictures made on the skin

3 houses built from blocks of ice

4 large animals that enjoy wallowing in muddy rivers

5 small insects that give you itchy bites

6 you use a camera to take these

p								
t					
i				
h					
m							
p					

Grammar

Headlines

Remember, **headlines** in newspapers and magazines are designed to attract the reader's attention and to give an idea of the content of the article. For example:

CARTER STRIKES GOLD!

Sometimes, headline writers use alliteration – a series of words that start with the same letter or sound. For example:

TOMB'S TREASURE TROVE

A Write three of your own headlines that could have been used by newspapers reporting Howard Carter's discovery. Include one alliterative headline. Try to make your headlines clever and eye-catching.

B Look at some newspapers. Copy three headlines that catch your attention. Under each, summarise the story being reported, and add a different headline that could have been used.

Sentence construction

Expanding sentences

Remember, sentences can often be **expanded** to make them more interesting or clearer, by adding words, phrases or clauses. For example:

The explorer found the tomb.

The <u>determined British</u> explorer, <u>Howard Carter, through dogged persistence and great effort</u> found the <u>incredible</u> tomb, <u>which had remained undisturbed for more than 3,000 years</u>.

When looking at a sentence that you have written, ask yourself questions to help you decide whether you need to add more detail. You can usually answer the following questions by adding **adjectives**, **adjective phrases** and **adjective clauses**:

What kind?   Which?   How many?   How much?

You can usually answer the following questions by adding **adverbs**, **adverb phrases** and **adverb clauses**:

When?   How?   Where?   How often?   For how long?

A Look at the sentences below. Write at least two questions about each one that would help you to expand them. The first one has been done to help you.

1 Carter had been searching for the tomb.

Which tomb?   For how long?

2 He was sure the tomb was in the valley.

3 Carter contacted his patron.

4 They opened the door of the tomb.

5 Carter felt happy.

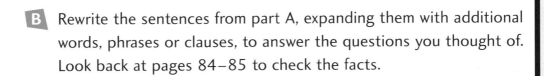

B Rewrite the sentences from part A, expanding them with additional words, phrases or clauses, to answer the questions you thought of. Look back at pages 84–85 to check the facts.

Writing

Magazine articles

The information about Howard Carter's discovery is set out in the style of a **magazine article**. Some magazines are about one particular subject, like football, cookery or computers. Other magazines are more general and have articles about many different subjects. No matter what sort of magazine it is, the articles in a magazine are there for two main reasons:

- to inform the reader
- to interest the reader.

The articles are the reason why people buy magazines. If they are not interesting and informative, nobody would buy the magazine!

Providing the reader with information

The writer of a magazine article has to research the subject, so that he/she can provide interesting facts. Remember the stages of non-fiction writing:

1	research	**2**	making notes
3	ordering the notes into paragraphs	**4**	writing a first draft
5	proofreading and revising	**6**	the final draft.

A 1   Look at the article on pages 84–85. In addition to the main explanation, what other information does the article give to help the reader to understand? Look at:

- the boxes
- the map
- the pictures.

Make some notes on how you think these help to inform the reader.

Capturing the reader's interest

Capturing the interest of the reader has a lot to do with how the information looks on the page. It has to look interesting in order to attract people to read it. A complete page of text doesn't look very interesting. You can make your writing more inviting to the reader by:

- using an eye-catching title
- using illustrations – maps, photographs, diagrams, drawings, etc.
- breaking the text up by using headings, boxes, different coloured backgrounds, etc.

2   Look again at the passage on pages 84–85. Make some notes about how the writer made the pages look interesting.

B 1 Look through some magazines and notice how the articles look on the page. Choose one that looks interesting and make some notes on why you would want to read that article. Compare it with one that you think is uninteresting.

2 Look carefully at the pictures below. They show some well-known achievements of the Ancient Egyptians. Choose one of the above topics to use as the subject of a magazine article.

• Ancient Egyptian hieroglyphics

• Felucca boats on the River Nile

• the Great Pyramid of Cheops

• the Sphinx at Giza

• the Temple at Abu Simbel

a Research your subject and make notes about it.

b Decide how you are going to set out your page.
  • Where will the text go?
  • Will you put some of the information in boxes?
  • What sort of illustrations will you have?

c Sketch a rough layout of the page, so you know what it is going to look like. You may be able to work on a computer.

d Write a first draft of your article, proofread and revise it and then write the final copy. Remember to include a title and a bibliography.

The Cat Family

These are some of the commonest members of the cat family:

Jaguar

Found in southern USA, Central and South America. Has a yellow coat marked with dark rosette-shaped spots and is about 2.5 m long. Lives in forests and scrub and can swim very well. Hunts peccaries (pig-like creatures), turtles, capybaras (very large rodents) and will attack livestock.

Wildcat

Found in Europe and West Africa. Approximately 75 cm long with a bushy rounded tail and thick, striped coat. Lives in dense woodlands.

Puma

Also known as the cougar, mountain lion or catamount. Found in North and South America. Is red/brown in colour, 1.5 m to 3 m long, slender and muscular. Its main food is deer but it will eat a variety of other animals.

Leopard

Found in Africa and Asia. Has a yellow coat, spotted with black rosettes. There are colour variations, such as the panther, which is black. Preys on monkeys, wild dogs and antelopes.

Snow leopard

Also known as the ounce. Inhabits the mountains of central Asia. Has a thick ash-grey coat marked with dark rosettes and is 1.9 m long. Hunts mountain goats, sheep and marmots (rodents).

Tiger
Found in central and southern Asia. Has a reddish-fawn coat with black stripes. Hunts at night, mainly killing antelope. Swims well.

Cheetah
Found in Africa and south-western Asia and is also known as the hunting leopard. Has a reddish-yellow coat with black spots and is 2 m long. It is the fastest mammal on Earth, reaching speeds of up to 110 kph.

Lion
Found mainly in Africa. Has a sandy-coloured coat and is 2.8 m long. Lives in grasslands.

Domestic cat
There is a large variety of breeds, thought to have developed from the African and European wildcat.

Comprehension

A
1 What is the snow leopard also known as?
2 Where are wildcats found?
3 Which is the fastest mammal on Earth?
4 Which members of the cat family can swim very well?
5 When does the tiger hunt?
6 What is the puma also known as?
7 In what type of landscape is the lion found?

Lions – the facts

Cats have fascinated humans for thousands of years. In Egypt about 3,000–4,000 years ago, all cats were worshipped as sacred animals, but it was lions that were particularly revered. The lion was believed to control the annual flooding of the River Nile, which was vital to the community because it enriched the

farmers' fields with fertile silt from the river. In many other early civilisations, the lion was linked with the sun. Its golden mane was thought to represent the sun's rays and the lion was a symbol of power and leadership.

As well as nobility and power, lions have also symbolised bravery in battle, watchfulness, courage and generosity. Unfortunately for the lions, however, Assyrian monarchs believed that they could only achieve true kingship by killing a lion – the king of beasts. They believed this would give them the strength and bravery of the lion.

In the third century BC, the Indian Emperor Ashoka, an early conservationist, erected many pillars inscribed with Buddhist teachings on nature and non-violence. The lion, sacred to the Buddhists, topped many of these columns.

Now, there are not many Asian lions left, either in India or elsewhere. A small population of about 300 in the north-west of the country is the only surviving group in the wild. Although very similar to its African relative, the Asian lion has a long fringe under its belly.

Like most of the cat family, the lion's sight has evolved to twilight hunting by becoming acutely able to detect slight movement in semi-darkness. They are also extremely sensitive to sound, being able to hear frequencies much higher than the human ear can detect. None of the cat family has a particularly well-developed sense of smell.

Lions have no natural predators except humans, who have, over the years, severely reduced lion populations through hunting and by reducing their natural habitats. However, where they still roam free, lions remain the monarchs, not only of the cat family, but of all the beasts.

Comprehension

 B Copy these sentences and choose the most appropriate words to complete them.

1 In early civilisations, the tiger/leopard/lion was linked with the Moon/Sun/Mars because of its head/mane/tail.

2 Only small numbers of Asian/European/African lions still exist, and the remaining 200/300/500 live in the north-east/south-west/north-west of India.

3 Lions' sight/hearing has evolved to allow them to hunt during the day/at twilight/at night.

C Write a few sentences to describe:
* the purpose
* the audience

of each of the two pieces of text.

Vocabulary

Similes

Remember, a **simile** is a way of describing something by comparing it to something else. Similes almost always include the word 'as' or 'like'. For example:

One of the kittens was <u>as timid as a rabbit</u> whilst the other was <u>as brave as a lion.</u>

A Similes are useful, but some common similes have been used so much that they are rather boring! Think of a new way of completing each of these well-known similes. You could use a word or a phrase.

1	as cunning as a fox	*as cunning as* _____
2	as fresh as a daisy	*as fresh as* _____
3	as slippery as an eel	*as slippery as* _____
4	as clear as glass	*as clear as* _____
5	as tough as old boots	*as tough as* _____
6	as pretty as a picture	*as pretty as* _____

B Choose three of the similes you wrote for part A and use each one in an interesting sentence of your own.

Spelling

Adding suffixes

Remember, to add a **suffix** to a word that ends with 'y' (where the 'y' sounds like the 'i' in 'tin'), change the 'y' to an 'i' and add the suffix. For example:

ugly   ugl<u>i</u>ness

A **1** Add the suffix 'ness', 'ment' or 'ly' to each word.

a *funny*	**b** *merry*	**c** *heavy*
d *haughty*	**e** *naughty*	**f** *silly*
g *pretty*	**h** *nasty*	**i** *gloomy*

2 Choose four of the words you made in part A and use them in sentences of your own.

B What class of word is each of the new words you made in part A?

Grammar

Word classes

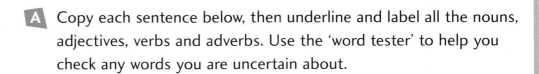

Remember, there are eight **word classes**, but the four most important are: **nouns**, **adjectives**, **verbs** and **adverbs**. For example:

The <u>elegant</u> <u>cheetah</u> <u>leapt</u> <u>effortlessly</u> into the <u>thorny</u> <u>tree</u>.

| adjective | noun | verb | adverb | adjective | noun |

A Copy each sentence below, then underline and label all the nouns, adjectives, verbs and adverbs. Use the 'word tester' to help you check any words you are uncertain about.

> **Word tester**
> Nouns: I noticed his/her/its _____ .
> Adjectives: This is very _____ .
> Verbs: He/she may _____ this.
> Adverbs: It was done _____ .

1   The three young lions greedily devour the meat of the huge zebra.

2   Vultures circle lazily overhead, waiting to swoop down and strip the carcass.

3   When tigers prowl through the vegetation of their natural habitat, their camouflage effectively makes them invisible to most animals.

Remember, another of the word classes is the **preposition**. Prepositions are important in showing the relationship (or 'position') of two things or people. For example:

The vultures waited patiently <u>in</u> the tree.

B 1   Copy the preposition from each sentence in part A.
   2   Write a sentence of your own that includes at least one of each of the following word classes: noun, adjective, verb, adverb and preposition. Neatly label each one.

Punctuation

Practising punctuation

In this section, you are going to practise using all the **punctuation** marks you have learnt in *Nelson English*. These are:

- full stops
- exclamation marks
- colons
- commas
- apostrophes
- semi-colons
- question marks
- speech marks

A Copy and correct each section of text below, adding the missing punctuation marks and capital letters. Be careful! They become increasingly difficult.

1 im really enjoying this visit to the wildlife park said jabbar

2 me too i am very excited about seeing the lions being fed replied wesley

3 what is a lions favourite meal jeev asked mr simmons

4 mr simmons said that he wasnt sure

5 speaking of food said jabbar isnt it time we stopped for lunch

6 as he ate jeev listed all the creatures they had seen so far his list included lions elephants giraffes monkeys snakes bears and chimpanzees

B Copy and correct the passage below, adding all the missing punctuation marks and capital letters. Remember to start a new line whenever the speaker changes, and look out for places where you might use a semi-colon instead of a full stop.

on the way back to school wesley was thinking about what it must be like to be an animal in captivity im pleased im not a wild animal he said to his friend alice who was sitting next to him why is that she asked rather surprised at such an unexpected comment well mused wesley it must be horrible not living in your natural surroundings keeping those lovely beasts in enclosures where they cant run and play just isn't right but

suggested alice in the wild many creatures are killed by humans
or die of starvation they have plenty of food in wildlife parks
thats not the point insisted wesley who felt very strongly about
the issue

Writing
Writing styles

You are going to write about big cats in two very different **styles**. The way you write needs to be different because each piece of writing has a different purpose. One piece of writing is going to be information writing, and the other is going to be personal writing.

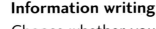

1 Information writing

Choose whether you will write:

- a report
- a fact file
- a magazine article
- a newspaper article
- an annotated diagram.

For information writing, you need to:

- research the facts
- make notes
- order your notes
- write your first draft
- proofread and revise your first draft
- present your final copy, including a title and a bibliography.

2 Personal writing

Choose whether to write:

- a diary extract
- a letter
- a passage including facts and giving your opinion.

Remember, you will need to:

- include your thoughts/feelings/facts/opinions/reasons
- write a first draft
- proofread and revise your first draft
- present your final copy.

Check-up

Vocabulary

A Use a thesaurus to find three synonyms for each word and its antonym (if it has one).

1 plenty   2 choose   3 ask   4 agree

B What is an eponym? Write three examples of eponyms.

C The following sentences are examples of hyperbole. What is hyperbole? Write what each sentence means.

1 It's enough to make your blood boil.   2 She seems to think she's the Queen.

D Write a sentence to explain the meaning of each of these proverbs.

1 Every cloud has a silver lining.
2 A rolling stone gathers no moss.
3 Don't count your chickens before they are hatched.

E Copy the words below. Underline the prefixes and write the number each prefix represents.

1 triangle   2 unicycle   3 hexagonal   4 centimetre

F Complete the following similes, then choose two to use in sentences of your own.

1 as hard as _____   2 as cool as a _____

3 as smooth as _____   4 as tight as a _____

Spelling

A Add the suffix to each word.

1 care + 'less'   2 pretty + 'ly'   3 excite + 'ment'

4 realise + 'ation'   5 release + 'ing'   6 naughty + 'ness'

7 package + 'ing'   8 gloomy + 'ly'   9 argue + 'ment'